Successful Shelves & Built-Ins

Successful Shelves & Built-Ins

Jay Hedden

STRUCTURES PUBLISHING COMPANY
FARMINGTON, MICHIGAN

Manufactured in the United States of America

Edited by Shirley M. Horowitz

Design by Carey Jean Ferchland

Cover photo courtesy of American Plywood Association

Current Printing (last digit)
10   9   8   7   6   5   4   3   2

Structures Publishing Co.
Box 1002, Farmington, Mich. 48024

Library of Congress Cataloging in Publication Data

Hedden, Jay W.
    Successful shelves & built-ins.
    Includes index.
    1. Built-in furniture. 2. Cabinet-work.
3. Storage in the home. I. Title.
TT197.5.B8H42 1979   684.1′6   78-27234
ISBN 0-912336-77-3
ISBN 0-912336-78-1 pbk.

Contents

You can add shelves in areas you never even thought of: above the kitchen sink to provide growing space for your herb garden, or above windows to store decorative cookware that is difficult to store in a cabinet. (Photo courtesy of Armstrong Cork)

1 Kitchen Cabinets

When you think of cabinets in a home, it's the kitchen that comes to mind first. This room almost always has the most cabinets, as well as cabinets with the greatest variety of functions.

Some kitchen cabinets contain a cooking range (cooktop), others the oven. Modern microwave ovens may be in a separate cabinet, or may share the same cabinet as the regular oven. Depending on the preference of the housewife—or perhaps the husband if he is a gourmet cook—the microwave oven may be above or below the regular oven

The sink is in a cabinet of its own, and may have a single, double or even triple basin. Some double-basin units will have one deep and one shallow basin, others will have basins of equal depth. If a sink includes a garbage-disposal unit, there must be a space under the cabinet to allow for it.

Automatic dishwashers are fitted under a countertop in a base cabinet, usually next to or very close to the sink. This allows for the shortest run of water pipes and drains.

PLANNING

Because so much work is carried out in a kitchen, planning its layout is the first and most necessary step when building kitchen cabinets. However, our aim is to tell you how to build those cabinets once you have determined the plan. For how to plan a kitchen layout, we suggest *Book of Successful Kitchens,* 2nd edition.

Timing

When remodeling a kitchen the sink counter should be completed first to enable its prompt use. This means that the line of base cabinets in which the sink is located will have to be completed, and the top installed, in a minimum of time. The family might be happy with one evening of dining out, or two, but when it becomes three evenings or more the situation can be inconvenient and expensive.

The second section to be worked on should be the cooktop, which may be in the same cabinet as the sink. You will probably not have to go without access to your cooking area for very long.

Dimensions

Before you start the cabinets for the sink, cooktop, range or oven, have specifications for these appliances. The instructions from the manufacturer show how the appliance is to be installed, and where the partitions and shelves must be located to allow the appliance to fit properly. An oven, for example, must be wired and fitted so it can be pulled out of its cabinet when work on it is necessary.

Some cooktop ranges are quite shallow, others are quite deep and may include a downdraft exhaust fan. Space must be allowed in the base cabinet below, as specified for the appliance.

As with any cabinet, kitchen cabinets are basically boxes; just make sure the boxes are the right size and shape.

Materials and Finishing

Basically, all cabinets are boxes . . . simple boxes. Plywood generally is used, and where it will show, the hardwood-veneered type is preferred. Interior partitions and shelves can be ordinary fir plywood, which helps keep down the cost.

Most kitchen cabinets are made of birch plywood. This is a light-colored wood, and fairly grain-free. It takes stain readily, and can be finished to

These birch cabinets have been finished with a dark walnut stain to the strong grain. For instructions, see page 9.

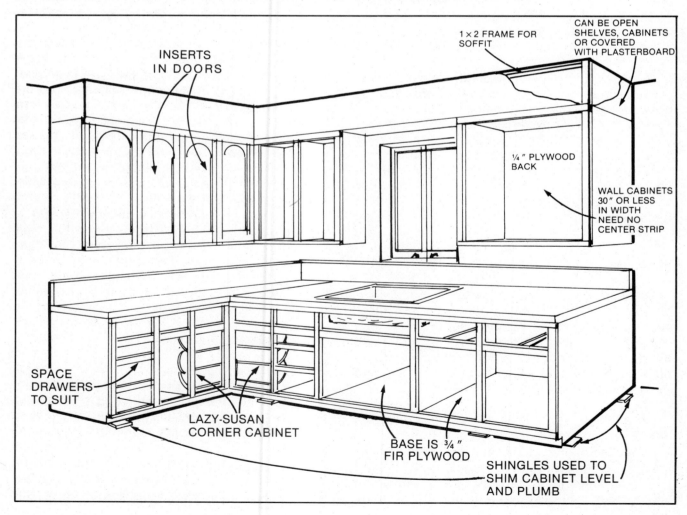

INSERTS IN DOORS

1 × 2 FRAME FOR SOFFIT

CAN BE OPEN SHELVES, CABINETS OR COVERED WITH PLASTERBOARD

¼" PLYWOOD BACK

WALL CABINETS 30" OR LESS IN WIDTH NEED NO CENTER STRIP

SPACE DRAWERS TO SUIT

LAZY-SUSAN CORNER CABINET

BASE IS ¾" FIR PLYWOOD

SHINGLES USED TO SHIM CABINET LEVEL AND PLUMB

simulate other kinds of wood. Birch plywood, as is the case with most hardwood-plywoods, has a "good" side and a "bad" or "off" side. That is, the one side is clear and straight-grained, while the other side may have some wild grain and perhaps stain streaks. We have found that using the "off" side can create some wonderful effects, because the strong grain gives an unusual character to the surfaces.

This character can be accented by using an unusual staining procedure: a bright green, blue, red or orange "decorator" stain is applied first. This type of stain actually is an analine dye, rather than an oil or water-based material. When the bright color has dried thoroughly, usually after 24 hours, a walnut penetrating sealer is applied.

The resulting finish is a dark walnut, with a gleam of green, blue, red or orange glowing through. The penetrating sealer not only provides the walnut color, but is a finish itself and no varnish or lacquer is required as a final coat. The brand we used is made by Watco-Dennis.

The most common way to build kitchen cabinets (and cabinets for other rooms) is to make them completely of ¾-in. plywood, with ends and partitions that sit on the floor. Dadoes are cut in the ends and in the partitions to accept shelves. Wooden cleats can be used to support shelves, or special shelf hardware (more expensive) can be installed to permit space adjustment between shelves.

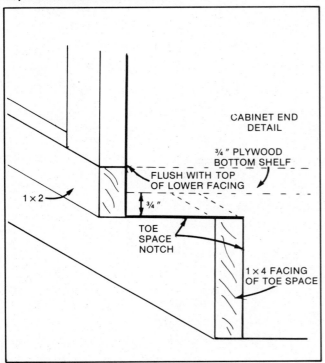

CABINET END
DETAIL

¾" PLYWOOD
BOTTOM SHELF

FLUSH WITH TOP
OF LOWER FACING

1 × 2

¾"

TOE
SPACE
NOTCH

1 × 4 FACING
OF TOE SPACE

CONSTRUCTION—BASE CABINETS

Base cabinets for a kitchen can be built in one of two ways. The first method is to build the cabinet using all ¾ inch plywood, with the cabinet ends and partitions the same height so all contact the floor. Shelves are fitted in dadoes cut in the inner faces of the ends, and on both sides of the partitions. Dadoes in the ends are ⅜ inch deep, which is half the thickness of the ¾ inch plywood. When shelves are in line on the partitions, the dadoes are 3/16 inch deep on each side, leaving ⅜ inch of plywood for support. When they are not in line, the dadoes should be the "standard" ⅜ inch deep.

The bottom shelf of the base cabinet, which actually is the bottom of the cabinet, is positioned 1 inch above the top of the toe-space notch. A full-length facing, cut from 1 × 2 stock, forms the bottom of the cabinet spacing and hides the space between the cabinet bottom and the lower ends of the partitions and the end uprights. Note that this piece of facing is part of the facing frame that is attached as a complete assembly.

There arises a potential problem at this point: the lower facing should be positioned so its upper edge is flush with the top of the bottom cabinet shelf. The ¾-inch thickness of the shelf and the 1-inch space between the shelf and toe space can add up to 1¾-inches. This is the width of the "old-fashioned" 1 × 2 (¾ × 1¾ inches). If you see some of the newer stock, a 1 × 2 will measure just ¾ × 1½ inches. Check the width of the 1 × 2 stock you buy and if it is only 1½ inches wide, make the dadoes for the bottom shelf only ¾ inch (rather than 1 inch) above the toe-space notch.

A length of 1 × 4 stock (which measures ¾ × 3½ inches) is nailed to the front edges of the ends and partitions of the base cabinet at the back of the toe space. This 1 × 4 is the "stretcher" that ties the ends and partitions together. It is easiest to face-nail the stretcher to the front edges of the partitions, but you might want the ends of the stretcher not to show at the end of the cabinet. In this case, make the toe-space notch in the cabinet ends ¾ inch shorter, back to front, than the notch in the partitions. Since the stretcher is cut shorter by the width of the ends, it will fit inside the ends. You then can nail through the ends of the base cabinet into the ends of the stretcher. Where one end of a base cabinet is against a wall, this modification could be made, of course, only on the open end. This might seem an obvious conclusion, but we'll say it now and repeat it every once in a while: measure twice and cut once. You can always shorten a piece of wood, but there is no practical way to lengthen it.

This same kind of "inside fitting" can be used at the lower back of a base cabinet for the 1 × 4 or 2 × 4 used there, and also for the 1 × 4 strip used at the upper back of a base cabinet.

Before joining the plywood ends and partitions, make dadoes for the required shelves. Or glue and nail 1 × 2 cleats to the inside of the ends and on both sides of partitions. If you want to spend a little more time and money, use shelf brackets that permit adjustment of the shelf levels.

The second basic construction method for kitchen base cabinets is to make a frame of 2 × 4s that sets on the floor and cover it with hardwood-faced plywood. The cabinet ends are nailed to it, as is the cabinet bottom. Partitions are cut to fit on top of the cabinet bottom. The front 2 × 4 for the floor frame is set back ¾ inch, so that a facing of 1 × 4 stock can be nailed to it. Stock 2 × 4s are not finished lumber, but are used as construction members. You can buy top-grade 1 × 4 stock for the facing used as the back of the toe space, or use a strip of hardwood-faced plywood, as used for the rest of the base cabinet.

The front-to-back members of the 2 × 4 frame are located at the ends, under each partition and about every 24 inches in between.

Arrangements for the shelves are the same as for the first type of cabinet construction.

The first type of cabinet generally has enough strength and rigidity to fit most situations, but the second type of construction is chosen when cabinets are built at one location and moved to another for installation. The 2 × 4 "chassis" assures that the cabinet assembly will not easily be racked or distorted out of shape. This also holds true when the cabinet is shimmed to be plumb and level when it is installed.

Shims used to level and plumb cabinets are ordinary second-course shingles. This kind of shingle is less expensive than first-course shingles. They may have knots and other imperfections, which make no difference as they are not seen, and they definitely are not seen when used as shims under cabinets.

Note that the cabinets are shimmed level and

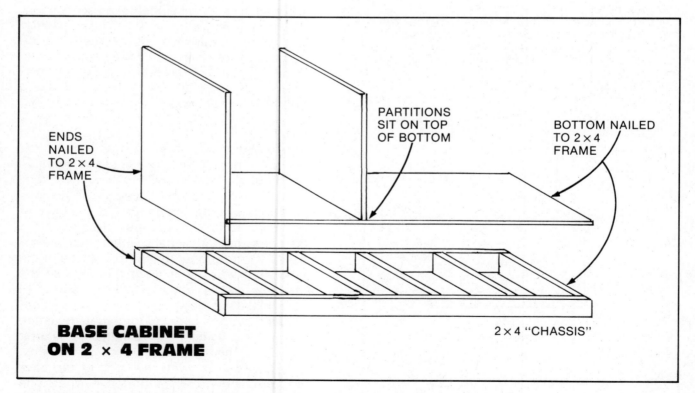

ENDS NAILED TO 2 × 4 FRAME

PARTITIONS SIT ON TOP OF BOTTOM

BOTTOM NAILED TO 2 × 4 FRAME

BASE CABINET ON 2 × 4 FRAME

2 × 4 "CHASSIS"

The second method of building cabinets is with a 2 × 4 "chassis" which provides rigid platform that allows cabinets to be moved from one location to another with minimum chance of racking or twisting.

plumb before the facing strip at the back of the toe space is applied. The strip then hides the shingles.

CONSTRUCTION—WALL CABINETS

Wall cabinets for a kitchen are simple plywood boxes, on the fronts of which are glued and nailed facing frames assembled from 1 × 2 stock. The assembly is much the same as base cabinets, including a back stretcher that usually is a 1 × 4. This stretcher provides a means of nailing or screwing the wall cabinets to the wall studs.

Cabinet Backs

In most cases, no backs are installed in kitchen cabinets. The wall of the house is the back of the cabinets. You might prefer to have a back of ¼ inch plywood or hardboard to prevent the relatively soft plasterboard (or plaster) from being damaged from items stored in the cabinets. This will require a ¼ × ¼-inch rabbet on the inner back edges of the ends of the cabinets, and parti-

tions will have to be shortened ¼ inch at the back to allow for the thickness of the plywood.

As previously stated, however, backs seldom are used in kitchen cabinets. If you buy ready-made cabinets, they will have backs. In this case, the backs help strengthen the assembly.

KITS

You also can purchase cabinets in "kit" form. That is, you get a box of pieces and parts that you take home and assemble with glue and screws or nails. The very practical reason for retailers selling these kits is that they have found that preassembled unfinished furniture of all kinds, including cabinets, are often damaged in shipping. Further damage can occur when the items are on display in the store. A flat package of material seldom is damaged, takes little storage space and is easy to carry home in the back seat of a car. It is said that a complete room of furniture can be carried in this form in the back seat and trunk of the family sedan.

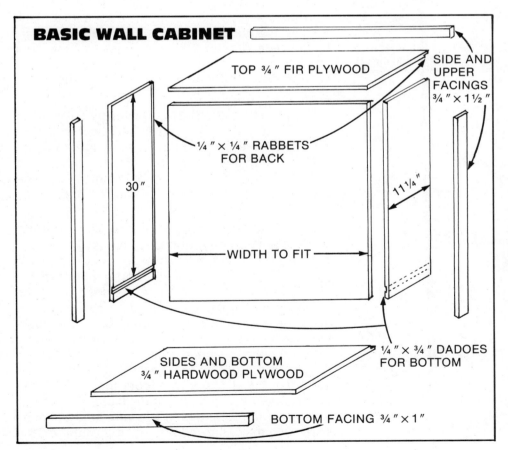

BASIC WALL CABINET

TOP ¾″ FIR PLYWOOD

SIDE AND UPPER FACINGS ¾″ × 1½″

¼″ × ¼″ RABBETS FOR BACK

30″

11¼″

WIDTH TO FIT

¼″ × ¾″ DADOES FOR BOTTOM

SIDES AND BOTTOM ¾″ HARDWOOD PLYWOOD

BOTTOM FACING ¾″ × 1″

Wall cabinets are simple plywood boxes with facing frames of 1 × 2 stock glued and nailed to them. Nailing strip can be used at back, or ¼-inch plywood can be set in rabbets to provide attachment.

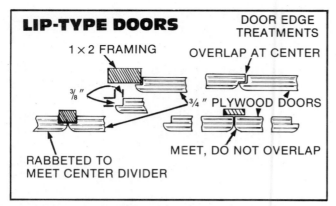

LIP-TYPE DOORS

DOOR EDGE TREATMENTS

1 × 2 FRAMING

OVERLAP AT CENTER

3/8"

3/4" PLYWOOD DOORS

RABBETED TO MEET CENTER DIVIDER

MEET, DO NOT OVERLAP

A lip-type door is the one most commonly used for base and wall cabinets. Various methods of fitting doors that meet in the opening are shown.

Cabinets in this pantry off the kitchen have overlay doors that cover framing, and touch almost edge-to-edge. Where drawers are installed above doors, fronts again almost touch, as do the doors below.

A flush-type door is hung in an opening, with just enough clearance to swing freely. Hinges are recessed into edges of door and frame; even "invisible" hinges can be used so that none show. (Photo courtesy of Azrock Floor Products)

We bring up these ready-made cabinets because one time- and money-saving way of installing even a roomful of cabinets is to combine ready-made units and cabinets you make yourself. You can match the doors and drawer fronts of the ready-made units by buying just doors and drawer fronts, and fitting them to cabinets you have built yourself.

CABINET DOORS

The overall styling of kitchen (and other) cabinets is largely determined by the doors and drawer fronts, plus decorative hardware and surface ornamentation. These various factors must be coordinated, of course, as you certainly would not use rustic early-American hinges with a French-provincial style of door or drawer front.

Types

There are four basic types of doors. All can be used on both wall and base cabinets.

The lip type that overlaps the frame all around. A rabbet is cut on the back edges of the door so the door is recessed half its thickness into the facer frame. The front edges of the door usually are rounded, but can be left square or even given a profile with a shaper or router.

The overlay type that completely covers the face of the cabinet, whether wall or base cabinet. Overlay doors are made larger than the opening, and the edges of adjacent doors and drawers meet. This type of door is quite heavy and places a strain on the hinges and framing.

The flush-type door hung in the opening with minimum clearance. There is just enough clearance for the door to swing freely to open and close. Hinges are recessed into the edges of the door and the frame. Because the doors must be fitted in the openings, they take more time to hang than other types. One variation of the flush-type is to cover the complete front of the cabinet with a sheet of plywood, then to cut the doors and drawer fronts out of the sheet with a jig saw or portable circular saw. The doors then are hinged in the openings and the grain matches exactly. Any minor irregularities in the cuts are not easily seen because the edges of the cuts match perfectly. Because of the extra work, however, and the chance of spoiling a full sheet of plywood, this type of door is not often seen. The method is also used when cabinets are made by applying wall paneling to a framing, as described in a later chapter, because the paneling is more easily cut and not as expensive as ¾ inch hardwood-faced plywood.

Sliding doors. Fine for some locations, such as above regular wall cabinets in what usually is a closed-in soffit, but only one half the cabinet is accessible when a door is opened. Still, where space is a problem, sliding doors for a cabinet might be the answer. Rabbeting the top and bottom of the doors permits them to fit together quite closely, minimizing entry of dust. When using power tools, make grooves in the top and bottom of the cabinet for the doors. The top groove should be twice the depth of the bottom groove so

the doors can be slipped into the top groove and then swung in and the bottom dropped into the lower groove. If you have only hand tools, make the tracks by nailing 2 strips of quarter-round molding to the top and to the bottom of the cabinet. A ¼ inch strip between the pieces of quarter-round keeps the doors from rubbing together. Height of the doors should be such that only about ⅛ inch projects up into the upper "track." Larger sliding doors are hung from metal brackets that run on an overhead track, utilizing ball-bearing wheels. Both single and double-track sets of this hardware are available. The single track is used where the door would open by sliding along the adjacent wall, rather than bypassing another door which is the case with double-track hardware. The door bottoms are kept plumb and aligned with a T-shape guide set in a hole in the floor. The guide fits in a groove cut in the bottom edge of the door.

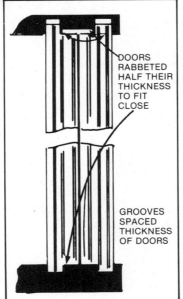

Rabbeting top and bottom of each door creates close-fitting sliding doors. The back edges of the front door are rabbeted, as are the front edges of the back door. This allows the doors to almost touch, so there is only a small gap that dust can enter. Be sure to seal edges, backs and fronts of doors.

DOORS RABBETED HALF THEIR THICKNESS TO FIT CLOSE

GROOVES SPACED THICKNESS OF DOORS

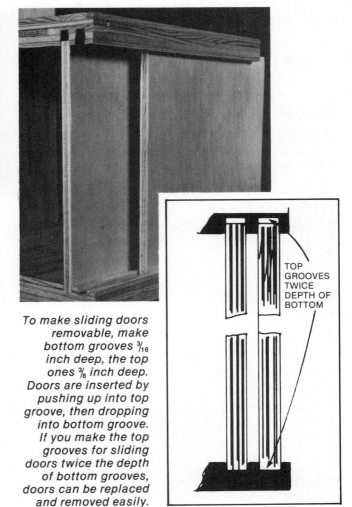

TOP GROOVES TWICE DEPTH OF BOTTOM

To make sliding doors removable, make bottom grooves ³⁄₁₆ inch deep, the top ones ⅜ inch deep. Doors are inserted by pushing up into top groove, then dropping into bottom groove. If you make the top grooves for sliding doors twice the depth of bottom grooves, doors can be replaced and removed easily.

Sliding Door Installation

If you have only hand tools, you can make sliding doors by spacing ¼-inch quarter-round molding on either side of a strip that is ¼ inch square.

Doors that run on tracks at the top are kept aligned at bottom by T-shaped devices fitted in holes in floor. T-shape fits in groove cut in bottom of door. If you have only hand tools, nail two lengths of quarter-round molding to floor to provide guide track. No center strip is required.

For easy-moving, by-passing sliding doors, you can use hardware that consists of two metal brackets fastened to the top of each door. Nylon wheels with ball bearings roll in a two-lipped track fastened to the door frame with screws. For a single door there is a one-lip track. This setup is generally used for larger cabinets and closets.

Styling

The surface appearances of cabinet doors and drawer fronts can be varied in a number of ways, and the look can be slab, raised or recessed panel, ornamental molding and many other styles. Doors and drawers can even have cloth, glass or plastic inserts. Woven cane, usually used for chair seats and backs, is another material that can be employed to make an attractive and unusual surface.

Metal inserts also can be used in a door. The metal is punched to simulate the colonial "pie safes" that were used for storage of pies and other foods to assure ventilation and minimize contamination by insects.

Inserts in the doors and drawer fronts of some "decorator" kitchens are covered with wallpaper that matches or is compatible with the paper on the walls. The inserts are made of thin hardboard or plywood and can be removed to permit replacing the covering when the kitchen is redecorated.

Door inserts are covered with wallpaper to match that on the wall. Panels in these doors are "raised" type, which means wallpaper would have to be stripped off when it comes time to redecorate the kitchen. Some doors have removable panels of hardboard or plywood that can be removed, to permit working on them more conveniently. (Photo courtesy of Thomas Strahan, Wallcovering Div. National Gypsum Co.)

For an unusual look in a colonial-style kitchen, door inserts are made of tin-plated steel or copper; patterns are punched with a nail or awl. These panels simulate panels used in antique pie safes. (Photo courtesy of Tile Council of America)

Construction

The most common cabinet door (and drawer front) is the simple lip-type slab with rounded edges and a rabbet on the back edges. The doors are made from ¾-inch plywood, generally with a hardwood veneer on the face, or from glued-up solid stock that has a net thickness of ¾ inch. The lip on the door overlaps ⅜ inch all around, which means the door must be ¾ inch longer than the cabinet opening, and ¾ inch wider. The same situation occurs for two doors that overlap across an opening that requires two doors. On one door the rabbet is reversed to match the rabbet on the other door where they overlap. A better arrangement is to have the doors meet on a stop strip, but not overlap.

The meeting edges need not be rabbeted, and can simply contact a stop strip; or, they can be rabbeted with a stop strip ⅜ inch closer to the front edge of the cabinet to keep the doors flush. Keep in mind that each door is only ⅜ inch wider than half the opening, to provide the ⅜-inch lip at the sides. The doors are a total of ¾ inch higher than the height of the opening, to provide for the upper and lower ⅜-inch lip.

Door edges can be shaped with a molding cutter on a table saw, a spindle shaper or with a por-

POPULAR DOOR STYLES

PLASTIC OR GLASS INSERT

SHAPED WOOD MOLDING WITH MATERIAL INSIDE

RAISED (OR RECESSED) PANEL

ROUTED PATTERN

Surface appearances of doors and drawer fronts may be varied in unlimited ways. Shown here are a few ways doors can be framed and inserts installed.

PANEL DOOR WITH GLASS OR PLASTIC INSERT

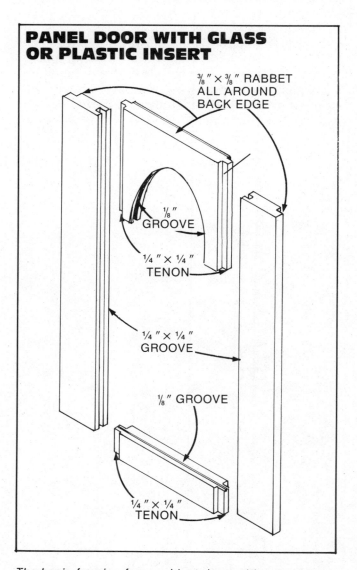

⅜″ × ⅜″ RABBET ALL AROUND BACK EDGE

⅛″ GROOVE

¼″ × ¼″ TENON

¼″ × ¼″ GROOVE

⅛″ GROOVE

¼″ × ¼″ TENON

The basic framing for a cabinet door, with some kind of insert, is shown. Top, bottom and side members of the frame can be varied to suit installation of various kinds of wood, metal, hardboard and plastic panels.

table router. After the edges are shaped, you can add interest by sawing or routing shallow grooves parallel to the edges, or by applying thin moldings.

Hardware

It's an easy job to install the special hinges made for lip-type doors. They are called ⅜-inch off-set hinges and are available in a wide variety of styles and finishes.

Latches come in several types, at several prices. Friction catches use rubber or plastic against metal to assure positive latching, and some types even are metal to metal; these are not too reliable, although inexpensive. Magnetic latches have the highest price, but are the most reliable. Be sure the magnetic latches you buy are the heavy-duty type. Light-duty magnetic latches have only about half the holding power of heavy-duty types, and should be used only on very small doors.

It is a waste of time and money to build a beautiful cabinet, then to install cheap hardware. Latches or catches must operate every day, many times in some instances, and if the catch fails, that is what will be noticed, not the beauty or craftsmanship of the cabinet.

Shutters

Shutters also can be used for cabinet doors. You can buy these ready-made in many sizes, and there is no reason why you cannot make them part of your cabinet. Fixed-louver shutters are the least expensive, of course, but do add a touch of style to your cabinets. Shutters with pivoting louvers are more costly, but are a good idea where ventilation is required for a cabinet.

A section of shutter with fixed louvers can be used for a drawer front, but shutters with movable louvers would be impractical.

If you examine shutters with fixed louvers you'll find that the frames are held together only by machine-driven staples in most cases, or by small nails. You can disassemble the shutter frame, remove the fixed-louver piece and cut it to the size you need. This fixed-louver member is a piece of wood with a flat back, and the front cut in sort of a "shingle" effect.

You can make your own fixed-louver stock, as indicated in the drawing. A dado blade in a radial-arm or table saw will help you do the job quite easily, and the width of the louvers, and their angle, can be made to suit the job.

After making the "shingles," cut rabbets along the four edges of the stock, flattening the angled

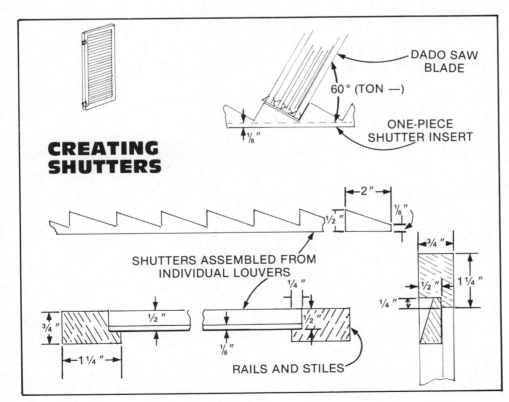

You can make your own fixed-louver shutter doors by cutting "shingles" in a piece of 1-inch softwood (¾ inch net), rabbeting edges to fit in grooves cut in frame of 1 × 2 stock.

17

For the bottle-glass look, use a transluscent plastic for safety reasons. This will also keep down weight, and minimize stress on door frame and hinges.

pieces, to create a thin edge that will fit snugly in grooves cut in the frames assembled from 1 × 2 stock. Don't glue the pieces in the grooves, rather let them "float" in the grooves so they can expand and contract with humidity changes. If you stain the parts of the shutter door before you assemble it, no unfinished wood will show as a result of the expansion and contractions—a touch of quality cabinetmaking that too often is missing on low-cost factory-made cabinets.

Bottle Glass

The use of "bottle glass" for cabinet doors seems to go in cycles. But using real glass can cause problems. It is quite heavy and the door frames must be heavily reinforced, and the hinges must be heavy-duty types. We recommend against real glass and suggest transluscent plastic with a bottle-glass pattern. The plastic is much lighter than glass, and will not shatter if struck with some object, like a heavy plate being removed from a cabinet.

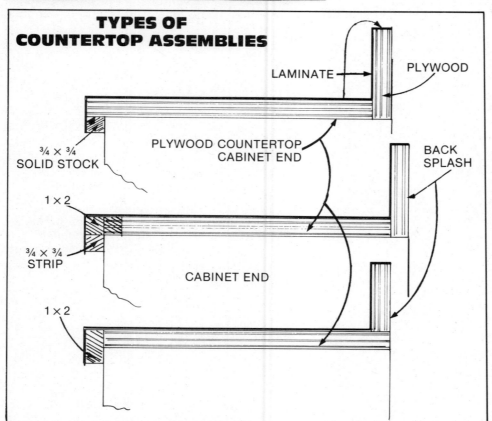

TYPES OF COUNTERTOP ASSEMBLIES

LAMINATE — PLYWOOD

¾ × ¾ SOLID STOCK

PLYWOOD COUNTERTOP CABINET END

BACK SPLASH

1 × 2

¾ × ¾ STRIP

CABINET END

1 × 2

Three of several different ways that cabinet countertops can be assembled. Assembly would be similar if ceramic tile were used instead of the plastic laminate indicated here.

CABINET TOPS

The "standard" width of the tops of kitchen base cabinets is about 24 inches. We say "about" because the tops are made by ripping a 4 × 8-foot sheet of plywood lengthwise. The resulting two strips will be 24 inches each, less half the width of the saw blade. The kerf of the usual saw blade is about $\frac{1}{8}$ inch, so each strip is about $23\frac{15}{16}$ inches wide. When a 1 × 2 is added to the front edge of the countertop to make it project by $1\frac{1}{2}$ inches, it becomes $\frac{3}{4}$ inches or more thicker. The additional $\frac{3}{4}$ inches (or more) makes the width of the counter "about" $24\frac{3}{4}$ inches wide, front to back.

If a backsplash of $\frac{3}{4}$-inch plywood is used, the actual countertop approximates the original 24 inches. There may be instances when a counter depth of more than 24 inches would be useful, say when a small microwave oven was set on it. There is no reason why you can't make the counter as wide as you wish, but there are practical limitations. A counter more than 24 inches deep will create cabinets underneath that are far too deep to be practical, at least just for storing items that must be reached.

A practical solution to the problem is to have slide-out shelves or slide-out bins. Any shelf that is made to slide out should have a rim around the edge or a back piece to keep things from falling off the back; in effect it would be a shallow bin.

Another obvious problem with making a countertop wider than 24 inches is that you are left with a long, narrow piece of plywood. This piece can, however, be ripped to 18 inches and used for the sides and shelves in wall cabinets.

Instead of adding 1 × 2s to the front edge of a cabinet top to make it project beyond the cabinets beneath, you may make the base cabinet $\frac{3}{4}$-inch (or more) narrower than the top. That is, cut the sides and partitions so the base cabinet is just $23\frac{1}{4}$ inches. Where space is a problem, this is the best answer. Remember, very few people can use the full depth of kitchen cabinets efficiently, so a matter of $\frac{3}{4}$ inch makes little difference.

Height

Standard height for kitchen base cabinets is 36 inches. This means that the ends and partitions should be $35\frac{1}{4}$ inches high, so when the $\frac{3}{4}$-inch plywood top is added, the total height will be 36 inches.

If the members of your family are shorter or taller than the average person, you might want to make the cabinets higher or lower than the standard 36 inches. But keep in mind that if you do not intend to stay in the house all your life, having cabinets 39 to 40 inches high for tall people, or 32 inches for short people, may restrict the resale of the house.

The solution to the problem is a compromise: build a couple high—or low—special counters for food-preparation centers or whatever the counter will be used for most. A low counter makes a handy baking center, as it is easier to knead bread dough or roll out pie crusts than on a standard height. A high counter suggests the use of a handy stool to ease kitchen work, such as peeling and cutting, or other chores that take a lot of time. Pull-out slabs make handy low counters and are great for blenders and mixers where the cook is working above the appliance. Locate such pull-outs about 30 inches above the floor; this is table height.

Tops for kitchen base cabinets should be purchased in one piece and installed after the

BACKSPLASH ON TOP OF COUNTER

24″

APROX. 24″

BACKSPLASH ON BACK OF COUNTER

24¾″

BACKSPLASH ASSEMBLY

A Pivot Counter Adds Space

One answer to the need for counters that are lower or higher than the "standard" 36 inches: slide-out or roll-out counter. This surface can slide in and out, or pivot, as shown in drawing below.

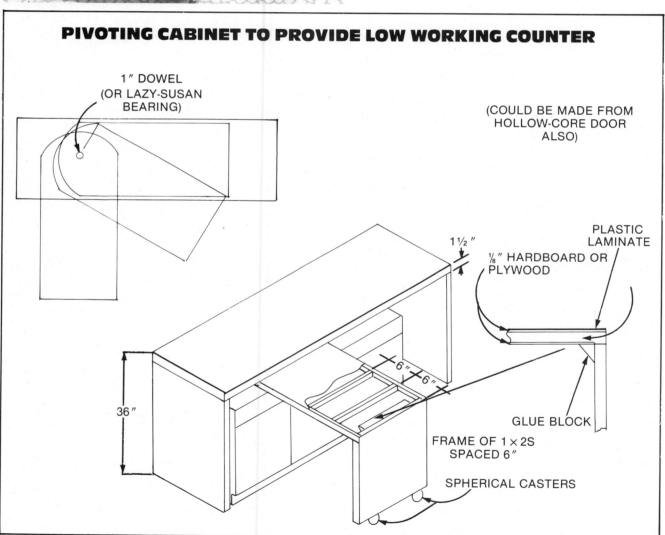

PIVOTING CABINET TO PROVIDE LOW WORKING COUNTER

1" DOWEL
(OR LAZY-SUSAN BEARING)

(COULD BE MADE FROM HOLLOW-CORE DOOR ALSO)

1½"

⅛" HARDBOARD OR PLYWOOD

PLASTIC LAMINATE

36"

6" · 6"

GLUE BLOCK

FRAME OF 1 × 2S
SPACED 6"

SPHERICAL CASTERS

Lift-off Shelf

Lift-off Shelf: One way to create a lower work surface for a shorter person is with a lift-off section of countertop. Lifting the section reveals a work surface covered with plastic laminate.

The L-shape section is reinforced with a triangular glue block between the front, which can be a false drawer front, and the top. The ends of the countertop exposed when the section is removed are covered with plastic laminate, as are the sides of the "well", to assure easy cleaning. The section of top is supported on 1 × 2 cleats fitted on each side of the well as indicated.

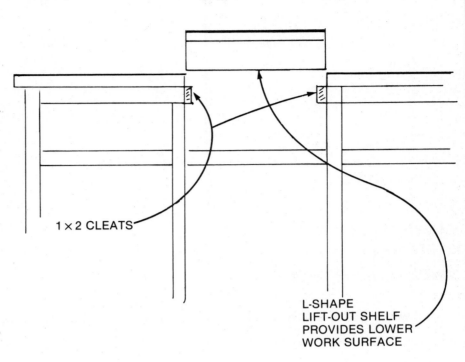

1 × 2 CLEATS

L-SHAPE LIFT-OUT SHELF PROVIDES LOWER WORK SURFACE

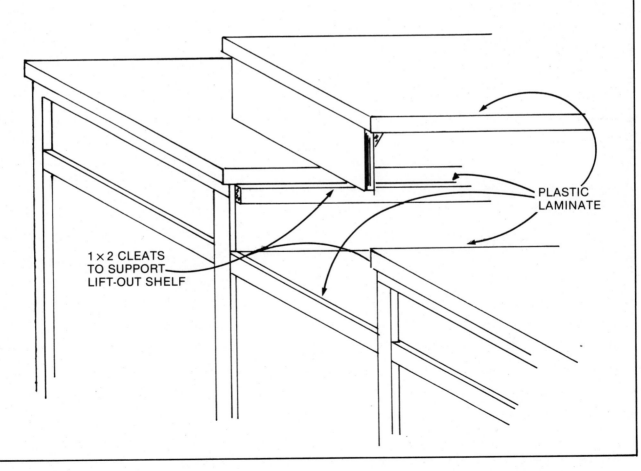

1 × 2 CLEATS TO SUPPORT LIFT-OUT SHELF

PLASTIC LAMINATE

cabinet is in place. Necessary joints can be made tight with devices made especially for this kind of assembly.

It is general practice, where possible, to cut the sink and other openings after the countertop is installed. In this case the plastic laminate (Formica, Micarta, Textolite, etc.) is applied after the countertop is in place. Openings for sinks, cooktops and other built-in appliances are cut after the plastic laminate is applied.

If one of the cuts is too close to the backsplash

to permit using the portable electric jig saw, then the top is first temporarily positioned and marked. It is then removed and the openings cut, and finally it is replaced and fastened permanently in place. In this situation the top would have to be fastened by driving screws from underneath, up through the framing into the top. Some tops are attached by driving screws down through the plywood top into the framing, then the laminate is applied over the top to cover the screws.

If a backsplash is to be installed *behind* the

SLIDE-OUT SHELF

A slide-out shelf can be installed to provide a lower working surface. This requires that one drawer be made shallower than the rest— which makes it handy for silverware. A 1 × 2 piece of framing is positioned horizontally across the opening so there is a slot a fraction higher than ¾ inch that has been created. The shelf is a piece of ¾-inch plywood or an edge-glued assembly of solid stock, made to fit the opening. Screw a small cleat to the underside of the shelf after it has been slipped into the slot, to act as a stop so the shelf cannot be pulled out all the way.

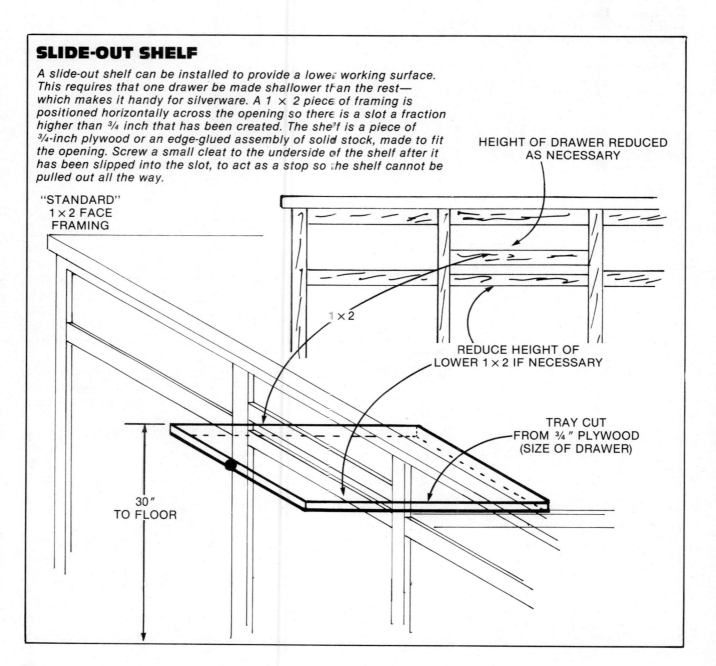

"STANDARD" 1 × 2 FACE FRAMING

HEIGHT OF DRAWER REDUCED AS NECESSARY

1 × 2

REDUCE HEIGHT OF LOWER 1 × 2 IF NECESSARY

TRAY CUT FROM ¾" PLYWOOD (SIZE OF DRAWER)

30" TO FLOOR

You can trim plastic laminate with special cutters in a portable electric router; however, inexpensive hand tools such as this Arlyn cutter, sold mail-order by Albert Constantine and Company (among others) does a neat job. It can be adjusted as necessary, and has replaceable cutters.

countertop, plastic laminate is applied to the splash before it is installed. This assures that the laminate will extend down behind the back edge of the countertop for a good seal. A metal or plastic strip can be fitted between the countertop and the back splash to assure a tight joint, although if the job is done properly, and the back edge of the countertop has been cut straight, the strips are not necessary.

Laminate

When plastic laminate is applied to a countertop, it is cemented to the front edge first, then trimmed to be flush with the upper surface of the top. This is called "self-edging." The laminate then is applied to the upper surface of the top so it overlaps the upper edge of the laminate on the front. This creates a joint that is horizontal, rather than vertical, so there is less chance of liquid entering the joint.

Contact adhesive is used to apply plastic laminate. If you have never applied laminate, it is suggested you apply it to some small projects first, before trying the cabinet. Basically, the contact adhesive is brushed on the wood countertop and on the back side of the laminate and allowed to set. Depending on the brand, the adhesive may

take 30 minutes or less to set. Read the instructions that come with the brand you by, as they will tell you the "working time" of the adhesive. Some types will be adhesive for one, two or three hours after they have been applied. Others will require application of a second coat after a certain length of time. This is no great problem if you do not apply the laminate within the specified time; just apply another coat of the adhesive to take care of the problem.

Brown wrapping paper and newspapers have been suggested for keeping the laminate and countertop separate until you have the laminate correctly positioned, and this system does work. However, you will find that sometimes paper will tend to stick to one or more spots in the adhesive. A better way is to use ⅛-inch dowels or small metal rods, such as gas-welding rods. When the laminate is properly aligned, you pull out the rods one at a time (also see Chapter 9, "Applying Plastic Laminate").

The front edge of the plastic laminate applied to the top is cut about ⅛ inch to ¼ inch too long, so it can be trimmed flush with the front edge after the laminate is firmly attached. There are devices that can be used with a portable router for trimming laminate, but inexpensive hand tools can also be used and they do an excellent job.

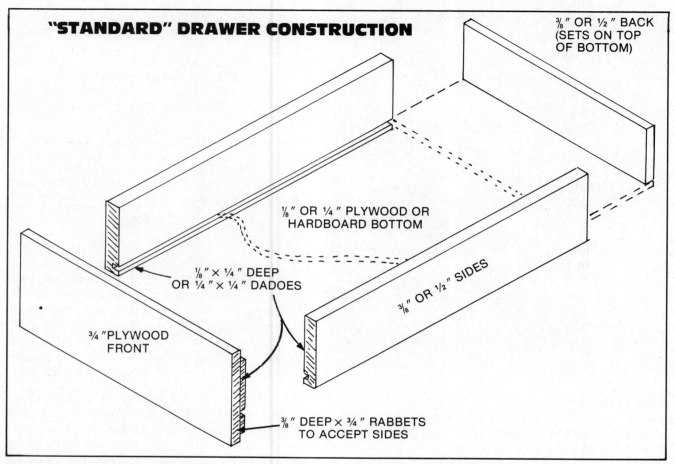

"STANDARD" DRAWER CONSTRUCTION

⅜" OR ½" BACK (SETS ON TOP OF BOTTOM)

⅛" OR ¼" PLYWOOD OR HARDBOARD BOTTOM

⅛" × ¼" DEEP OR ¼" × ¼" DADOES

⅜" OR ½" SIDES

¾" PLYWOOD FRONT

⅜" DEEP × ¾" RABBETS TO ACCEPT SIDES

The standard method of making drawers for cabinets (and other pieces of furniture) is detailed. Front and sides of drawer are grooved to accept bottom that "floats" in grooves. Drawer back sets on top of the bottom, is held with just a couple of brads.

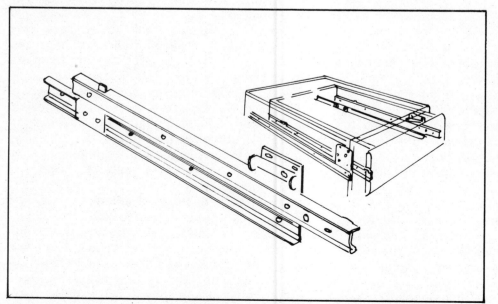

Drawers that carry only lightweight items can simply slide on a flat shelf of plywood, or have simple wooden guides on underside. Most drawers, however, need some kind of mechanical slides, with heavy drawers being fitted with ball-bearing extension guides.

There is no need to buy an expensive power tool if you are going to do only one counter job.

Contact adhesive grips immediately, as has often been stated, but not instantly. That is, if you are just a bit out of line, gently push the laminate in the direction you want to move it. Contact adhesive has a rubber base and it will give a bit. In an extreme case, where you have really slipped out of line, gently raise the laminate and cut away the stringy connections made by the adhesive between the laminate and the countertop. If you have cut away too much of the adhesive, you would do better to peel the laminate free of the countertop and apply another layer of adhesive to both surfaces and then redo the job.

If you will use a ceramic tile on the countertops, apply with mastic, and seal the joints with grout. Openings are always cut prior to installation of the countertop. With ceramic tile, the hardest area to cut and fit is the back row of tiles. The front edge of the countertop is trimmed with L-shaped pieces of tile especially made for the application.

DRAWERS

Drawers for kitchen cabinets are assembled in a number of different ways, but the "standard" method (illustrated) is the best. The front and sides of the drawer are grooved to accept the bottom that generally is ⅛ inch or ¼ inch hardboard or plywood, and the back of the drawer sets on top of this bottom. The bottom is held only by a few brads or small nails driven up through it into the back. This allows the bottom to "float" as it expands and contracts with humidity instead of forcing the drawer apart. Make sure there is a bit of clearance all around the bottom—it should be a loose fit in the dadoes—so it can expand and contract.

A number of devices are used to make drawers slide more easily; they range from simple projections of nylon or other plastic to ball-bearing slides. Cost is the factor to consider here; that, and how much the drawers will be used. Weight also is a factor; a drawer that will be loaded with heavy pots and pans, for example, definitely needs a smooth-working slide of some type. A lightweight drawer such as used in a kitchen desk, and which will hold only paper, could be installed with no slides at all. A simple centering guide would do the job.

Be sure to have the slides on hand before you start the assembly of the drawers. Check the instructions to determine the required clearances. Most popular ball-bearing slides require about ½ inch clearance on each side, which means the overall width of the drawer will have to be reduced 1 inch. Some center-type guides call for the front-to-back depth of the drawer to be reduced by ½ inch or more—read the instructions.

Where possible, make all the drawers the same size. This means it will take only a little more time to make a dozen than to make one or two. This is not always possible, of course. Some base cabinets are drawers from top to bottom, and require several sizes with the larger ones on the bottom.

With a little planning it is possible to make all the drawers above the doors in the base cabinet the same size. The fronts of some corner base cabinets—behind which a lazy-Susan is installed—sometimes are fitted with full-length doors and no drawers. That is, no drawer is fitted just under the countertop. Your design might look a lot more uniform, however, if you make a "false" drawer on each door for such a corner cabinet.

CORNER CABINETS

When making a corner cabinet, the first decision is to determine what size it will be. The cabinet can be built to the full 24-inch depth, as the other cabinets adjacent to it, or it can be made shallower to conserve lumber and space. The largest circular shelves are 28 inches in diameter, and this will not quite fill the available space in the corner. Each door, however, would have to be made a full 18 inches wide for this larger circular shelf. There is no really good reason for making the corner cabinet very wide, because the space can be better utilized for regular cabinets.

As shown in the drawing, keeping the cabinet doors to 12 inches wide will allow using a 22- or 24-inch diameter shelf and the cabinet will be a practical size. Build the cabinet to the dimensions shown. Note that the top and bottom shelves are the same size, and ¾ inch longer in both dimensions to allow for the ⅜-inch projections into the ⅜-inch dadoes cut in the sides at the bottom, and the rabbets at the top.

Install the lazy-Susan hardware as per the instructions that will be packaged with it. Glue and nail the facing strips of 1 × 2 stock, after carefully measuring. Both doors are the same height, but one is ¾ inch narrower than the other to allow for the ¾-inch thickness of the door in front. Doors are fastened directly to the angles in the notched shelves—which can be purchased metal or cut from plywood—with wood screws.

Edges of the doors must be slightly beveled to permit their slipping past the front trim. You can purchase positioning stops to hold the doors in the closed position, so they will be flush with the rest of the cabinet doors.

Finish the toe space of the cabinet to match that of the other cabinets; this can be done after all the cabinets are installed. Note that the corner cabinet is screwed to the adjacent cabinets, or you can use nuts and bolts. Cleats are fastened to the wall near the corner to provide support for the cabinet top.

Corner cabinets are fitted with a set of lazy-Susan shelves to utilize all storage space. Doors are kept to 12 inches wide, as wider cabinets would waste space. Hardware is available to permit making your own wooden shelves, or you can buy premade metal shelves with a cutout that fits corners.

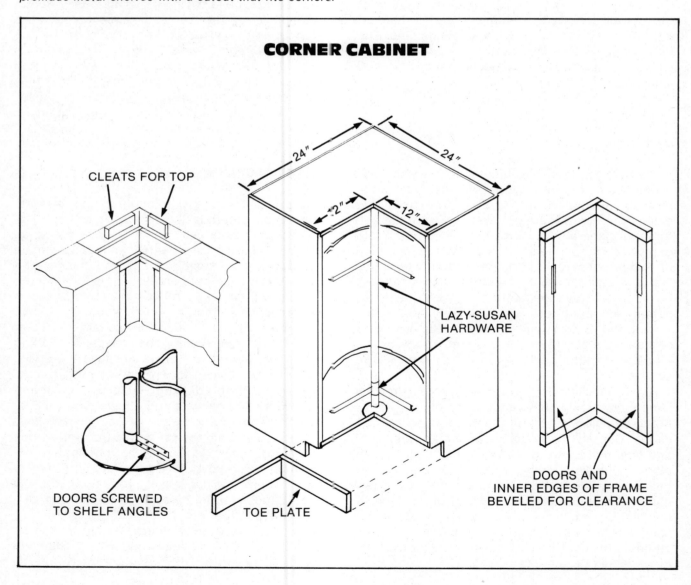

CORNER CABINET

CLEATS FOR TOP

24" 24"

2" 12"

LAZY-SUSAN HARDWARE

DOORS SCREWED TO SHELF ANGLES

TOE PLATE

DOORS AND INNER EDGES OF FRAME BEVELED FOR CLEARANCE

Installing Your Cabinet

1

Cabinets must be attached to studs for full support. Studs are usually located 16 inches on center. Locate studs with stud finder, tapping with hammer or nail driven through plaster at height that will be hidden by cabinets. Cabinets must always be attached to walls with screws. Never use nails!

2

Cabinets must be installed perfectly level — from a standpoint of function as well as appearance. Find the highest point of floor with the use of a level.

3

Using a level or straightedge, find the high spots on the wall on whcih cabinets are to be hung. Some high spots can be removed by sanding. Otherwise, it will be necessary to "shim" to provide a level and plumb installation.

4

Using the highest point on the floor, measure up the wall to a height of 84 inches. This height, 84 inches, is the top height of wall cabinets, oven and broom cabinets.

5

On the walls where cabinets are to be installed, remove baseboard and chair rail. This is required for a flush fit.

6

Start your installation in one corner. First assemble the base corner unit, then adding one unit on each side of the corner unit. This — as a unit — can be installed in position. Additional cabinets are then added to each side as required.

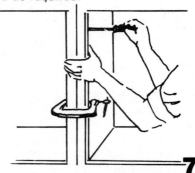

7

"C" clamps should be used in connecting cabinets together to obtain proper alignment. Drill 2 or 3 holes through ½ inch end panels. Holes should be drilled through to adjoining cabinet. Secure T-nut and secure with 1½ inch bolt. Draw up snugly. If you prefer you may drill through side of front frame as well as "lead hole" into abutting cabinet, insert screws and draw up snugly.

8

Each cabinet — as it is installed to the wall — should be checked front to back and also across the front edge with a level. Be certain that the front frame is plumb. If necessary, use shims to level the cabinets. Base cabinets should be attached with screws into wall studs. For additional support and to prevent back rail from "bowing," insert block between cabinet back and wall. After bases are installed cover toe kick area with material that is provided.

9

Attach countertop on base cabinets. After installation, cover countertops with cartons to prevent damage while completing installation.

10

Wall cabinets should then be installed, beginning with a corner unit as described in step #6. Screw through hanging strips built into backs of cabinets at both top and bottom. Place them ¾ inch below top and ¾ inch above bottom shelf from inside of cabinet. Adjust only loosely at first so that final adjustments can be made.

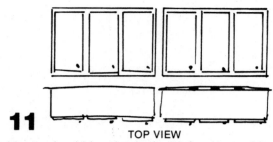

11

TOP VIEW

Wall cabinets should be checked with level on cabinet front, sides, and bottom to insure that cabinets are plumb and level. It might be necessary to shim at wall and between cabinets to correct for uneven walls or floors. After cabinets and doors are perfectly aligned, tighten all screws.

This sequence is from the installation manual of Kitchen Kompact, a giant of the industry.

Problem Doors

There are very few "perfect" conditions where floors and walls are exactly level and plumb. Therefore, it is necessary to correct this by proper "shimming" so that the cabinet is not racked or twisted and so that cabinet doors are properly aligned.

The top left hand corner is pulled into a low spot on wall. A shim is needed between cabinet and wall at this point.

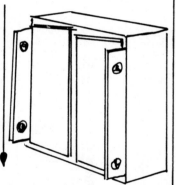

Before: Doors are out of line. Cabinet is racked.

TOP VIEW

Detailed line reveals top edge of cabinet slightly out of line.

Use level to see if cabinet face is plumb on both edges. Same condition exists if lower right hand corner of cabinet is against a high spot on wall. Remove the high spot (by sanding) or shim other three corners.

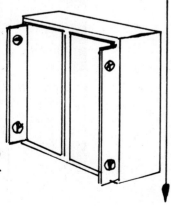

After: Doors are aligned properly. Cabinet is plumb and level.

SHIM

TOP VIEW

2 Bookcases and Shelves

Bookcases and book shelves are basically built in much the same way as cabinets, but usually need to be stronger because of the considerable weight of books. The styling differs from that of cabinets . . . you may have doors that conceal the lower shelves, while the upper shelves will be open. Additionally, the lower cabinet must support not only the weight it contains, but the top cabinet plus all the books (and possibly statuary, vases, etc.) and magazines it will hold.

CONSTRUCTION TIPS

To strengthen the lower cabinet, include partitions spaced no more than about 3 feet apart. The problem is that a space less than 3 feet will not hold many books or other items, so you may want to reinforce the upper portion of the cabinet to permit the span of 3 feet or more.

This is done by using a facing 1 × 4 stock across the top of the base cabinet, rather than the usual 1 × 2. The facing then hides a 2 × 4 that is fitted across the top of the cabinet. It makes the cabinet more rigid and also supports the plywood top on which the upper book case rests.

Note that the partitions are notched to fit around the 2 × 4's, one being located at the back and one at the front. A bookcase such as shown can be used either as a unit against the wall, or free-standing in a room to create a room divider.

If it is the latter, you might want doors on both sides of the lower cabinet, to provide access from both sides. By the same reasoning, you will want

These book shelves are combined with cabinets below. They are "architectural" in that they were built when the house was constructed, and are styled to match the fireplace. Shelves are adjustable, with clips in holes in the side pieces.

Built-in Book Shelves (Utilizing a Recessed Wall)

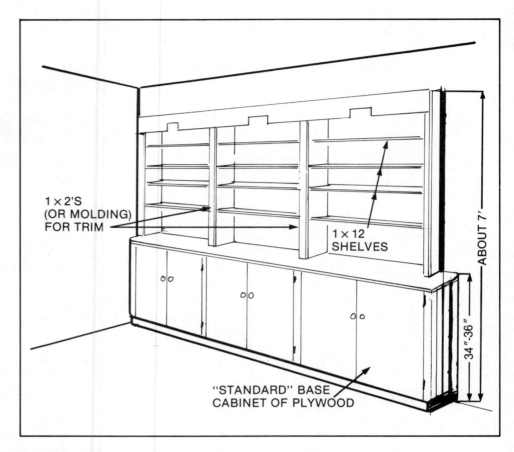

1 × 2'S
(OR MOLDING)
FOR TRIM

1 × 12
SHELVES

ABOUT 7'

34"-36"

"STANDARD" BASE
CABINET OF PLYWOOD

BASE CABINET FOR BOOKCASE

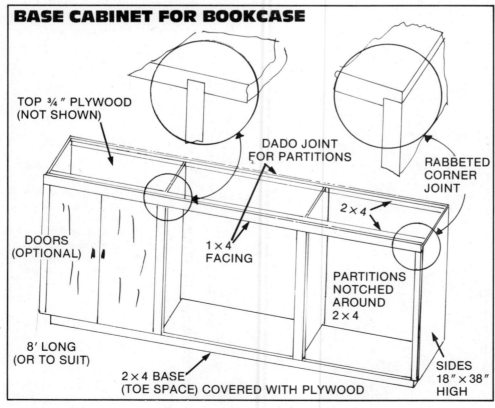

TOP ¾" PLYWOOD
(NOT SHOWN)

DADO JOINT
FOR PARTITIONS

RABBETED
CORNER
JOINT

2 × 4

DOORS
(OPTIONAL)

1 × 4
FACING

PARTITIONS
NOTCHED
AROUND
2 × 4

8' LONG
(OR TO SUIT)

2 × 4 BASE
(TOE SPACE) COVERED WITH PLYWOOD

SIDES
18" × 38"
HIGH

A base cabinet for book shelf/cabinet has a reinforced frame with 2 × 4s or 2 × 2s across the top to support the plywood top. The cabinet can be used as a wall unit, or as a room divider, and doors can be fitted on both sides of the base cabinet.

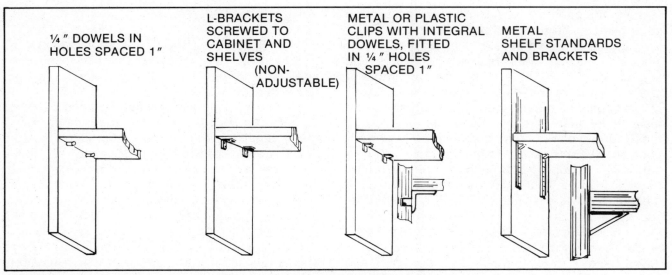

¼" DOWELS IN HOLES SPACED 1"

L-BRACKETS SCREWED TO CABINET AND SHELVES (NON-ADJUSTABLE)

METAL OR PLASTIC CLIPS WITH INTEGRAL DOWELS, FITTED IN ¼" HOLES SPACED 1"

METAL SHELF STANDARDS AND BRACKETS

Shelves can be fixed rigidly in dadoes, or with metal angle brackets, or made adjustable by several devices.

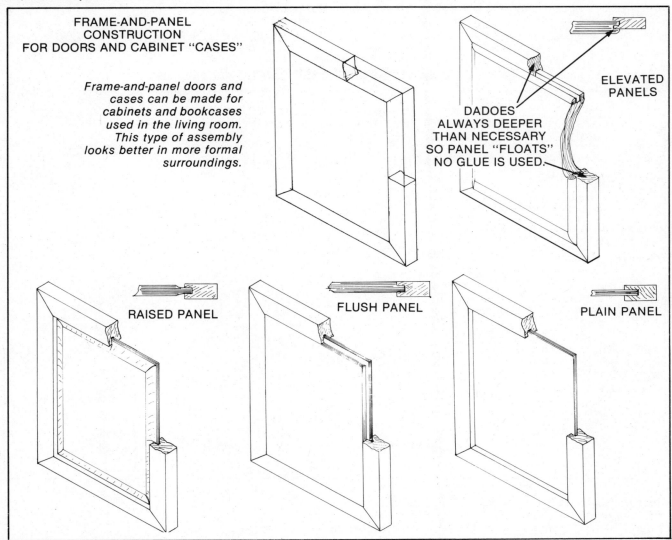

FRAME-AND-PANEL CONSTRUCTION FOR DOORS AND CABINET "CASES"

Frame-and-panel doors and cases can be made for cabinets and bookcases used in the living room. This type of assembly looks better in more formal surroundings.

DADOES ALWAYS DEEPER THAN NECESSARY SO PANEL "FLOATS" NO GLUE IS USED.

ELEVATED PANELS

RAISED PANEL

FLUSH PANEL

PLAIN PANEL

to make the open shelves at the top wide enough so books can be fitted on both sides, thus in effect, doubling the amount of shelf space.

Most hardback books are about 8½ inches high and about 6 inches wide. If you have a number of reference books, encyclopedias and the like, they will of course be bigger and you will either have to make wider shelves (deeper) or figure on inserting these larger books from only one side of your book shelves. Where this is the case, it might be a better idea to apply paneling to the one side of the room divider, particularly if the room is paneled. If it is not, and there is wallpaper on the room walls, you can apply smooth hardboard to the back of the book shelves and cover it with the wallpaper or wallcovering used on the room walls.

The base of the lower cabinet should be made of 2 × 4s also, to provide the needed strength, and the lumber then is covered with strips of the hardwood-plywood used for the cabinet.

Adjustable Shelves

If you have a variety of sizes of books, and most people have, it's a good idea to make the shelves adjustable. They then can be spaced to accept any size of books you have.

There are a number of ways this can be done. First, drill a series of holes in the side pieces of the cabinet in which short lengths of wooden dowel are inserted to support the shelves. Space the holes about 1 inch apart. The same kind of spacing of holes is done for metal or plastic clips you can buy to support the shelves. The projecting dowel portion of the clips is ¼ inch, so make the holes that size.

A bit more expensive, but very attractive and strong, are shelf standards into which brackets are snapped. The spacing for these standards is a bit less than 1 inch, so you can adjust for any size book or decorative item you want to display.

Book Shelves to Fit on Base Cabinet

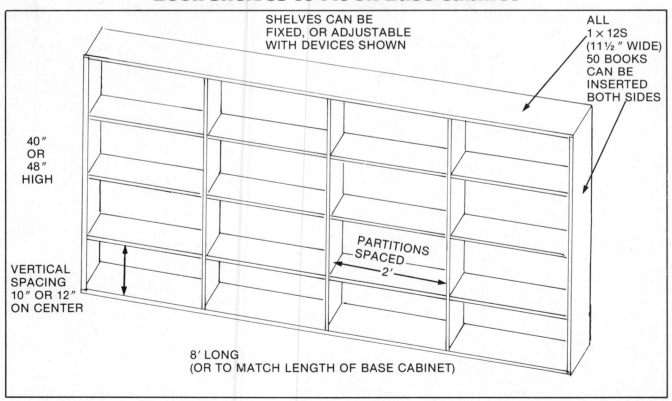

Simple shelving is made to rest on base cabinet, and it also can be used as a wall unit or room divider. If used as a wall unit, shelves could be 1 × 8s or 1 × 10s; shelves shown would allow a standard book to be inserted on both sides.

Shelves installed by the homeowner have an "architectural" look, as they were assembled in a recess in the wall, then painted to match the wall. Shelves are cut from plain pine shelving. (Photo courtesy of Armstrong Cork Co.)

Because bookcases or bookshelves will be in a living room or other more formal room, doors will be more decorative than those used for kitchen cabinet. The frame-and-panel type are good, and four examples are shown here in cross-section. The rails, of course, are solid stock, while the panels for the plain and flush doors can be plywood.

Stock for projecting or raised panels should be solid lumber, either hardwood or softwood. The sides and backs of the cabinets that have been made as bookcases, or bookshelves also can be frame and panel (also see chapter 7 for an example of paneled cabinets).

Simple Shelves

The simplest kind of bookcase or bookshelf is one assembled from straight-grained pine shelving which is installed, then painted or stained. Painting is the usual way that shelves are finished if they are to be installed as an architectural part of a room.

When we say "architectural," we mean quite literally that the shelves are part of the basic structure of the room. A recess in a room, or a niche — say alongside a fireplace — is the most common location for such bookshelves or bookcases. The shelves can be supported by any of the devices previously described, if the vertical members of the assembly are wood. The devices cannot be used, of course, in a plaster or plasterboard wall, as these materials simply will not support much weight in shear, especially when the devices are quite small.

If the shelves are to be fixed, then you simply cut dadoes across the vertical members and insert the shelves. In the case of a recess or niche, build the assembly so that when the shelves are inserted in the dadoes, they force the vertical pieces tightly against the sides of the recess or niche.

SPECIALTY SHELVES

Corners

If you can only locate the bookcase in a corner of the room, you can try a corner cabinet although the shape of such a cabinet does not really lend itself to holding books. One answer to the corner cabinet is to utilize book ends at the end of each row of books then place some kind of decorative item beside each book end, adjacent to the slanting or angled side of the case.

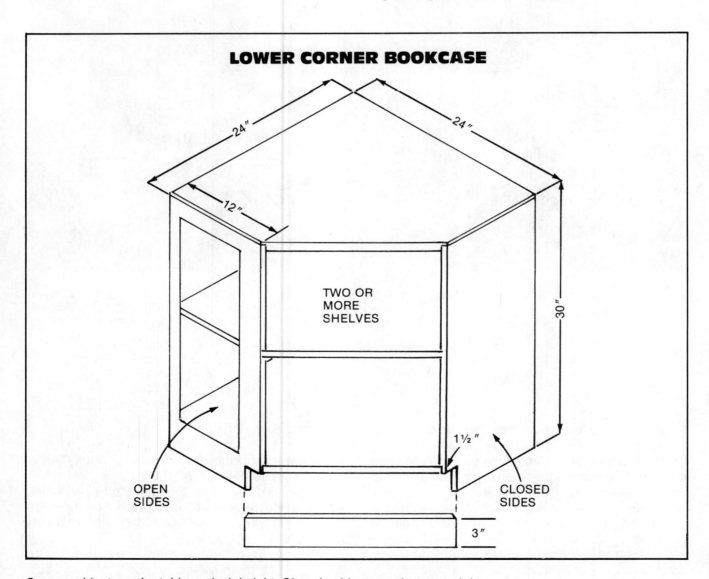

LOWER CORNER BOOKCASE

24"   24"

12"

TWO OR MORE SHELVES

30"

1½"

OPEN SIDES

CLOSED SIDES

3"

Corner cabinet can be table or desk height. Closed cabinet, as shown on right side, is not handy for books. Left half of cabinet has open construction. More shelves can be installed, of course. This cabinet can be made square for chairside use.

Corner Cabinet Construction

ALL ¾" PLYWOOD
EXCEPT AS NOTED

A corner cabinet can utilize space in a corner of the room, but this is not too handy for books. This cabinet has pieces "A" and "B" cut from 3/4-inch plywood or 1-inch solid stock, then dadoed as indicated. All shelves are cut to same size; all angles are 45 degrees at back and edge. Trim can be shaped to suit, as can "pediment" at top—shown with triangular shape. Pieces of 1/4-inch plywood are cut to fit between "A" and "B" pieces after shelves are fitted in dadoes. You can install doors on lower part of cabinet, or eliminate them.

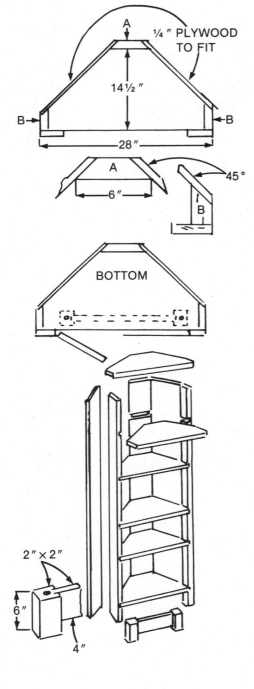

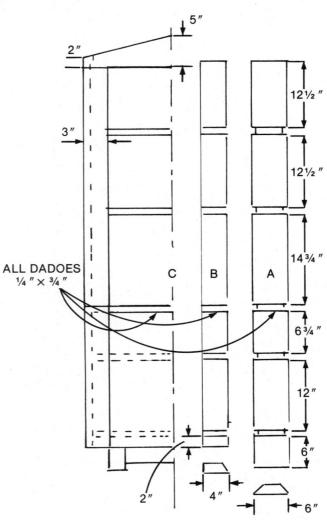

Where room is even more restricted, you might consider a small bookcase that doubles as an end table. A pair of these bookcases can be used at either end of a couch, or one can be used beside each of a pair of easy chairs in a living room.

Where only a few books are to be made available, you can have one or two shelves in a chairside bookcase, with a storage cabinet beneath. Paperback books and magazines can be stored in the cabinet, as they do better when placed flat, rather than being stood on end where they bend and wrinkle.

Another corner possibility is a corner seat with a window shelf. Use a bright and cheerful wallcovering on the upper walls, a matching fabric on the cushions of the built-in seat, and a contrasting wallcovering on the lower part of the built-in. Molding adds a nice touch, and

underneath the cushions there are lift-up plywood covers that conceal all kinds of storage.

Living Rooms

Although you probably do not have a fabulous circular living room with a soaring chimney above the fireplace and a huge skylight that lets in the sun in the daytime and displays the stars at night, note that even in the sumptuous setting shown on page 39, there are shelves and built-ins.

The walls are lined with open shelves, and alongside there are drawers for storage of all sorts of things. The built-in seats are attractive and comfortable, but offer even more storage. The seats lift up to expose chests, while the backs of the couches tip down (after the seat cushions are removed) to expose more shelves.

You can fill more than one need by using this plan. This "L" shaped bench hides plenty of usable storage space and could be adapted to any room in the house. The matching wallpaper and fabric makes it appear built-in.

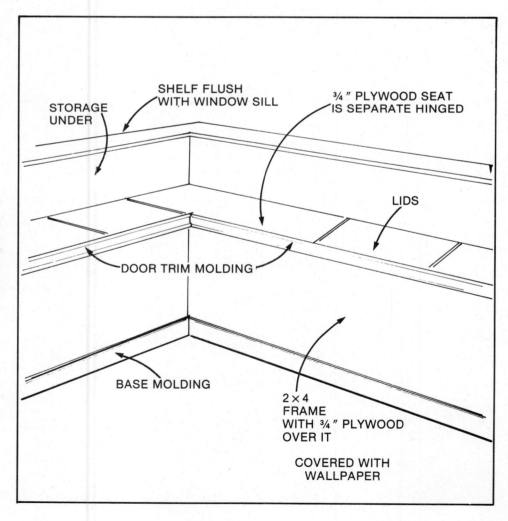

STORAGE UNDER

SHELF FLUSH WITH WINDOW SILL

¾″ PLYWOOD SEAT IS SEPARATE HINGED

LIDS

DOOR TRIM MOLDING

BASE MOLDING

2 × 4 FRAME WITH ¾″ PLYWOOD OVER IT

COVERED WITH WALLPAPER

Although it is not likely you'll have such a living room, why not adapt some of the ideas you see in it? A wall can be formed into three or more planes; you can build seats with storage under them, and shelves behind and above them. The resulting triangular spaces behind the seats can be utilized on the opposite wall for closets or other storage areas.

The resulting living room may be smaller, but since the majority of the furniture is built-in, you'll have more open floor space.

Where you have a simple decor in a living room, a simple built-in is appropriate. The L-shaped unit on page 40 serves as a table behind the couch. Along the wall it can be a shelf for the indoor gardener or, if placed at the very end, it is a spot for the ubiquitous television set.

The table is made by glue-laminating two thicknesses of plywood together, and it's supported on one end by a "leg" made in the same manner. A cleat on the wall supports the other end, and the cleat extends along the wall to hold up the shelf. The end of the shelf is supported on another leg of doubled plywood, and the front edge of the shelf is stiffened by a strip of 2 × 4 to which the plywood is glued and screwed.

Even a very modern and glamourous living room needs built-ins. This room has storage under and behind the seats, as well as in cabinets, drawers and bookshelves above the seats. (Photo courtesy of Tile Council of America.)

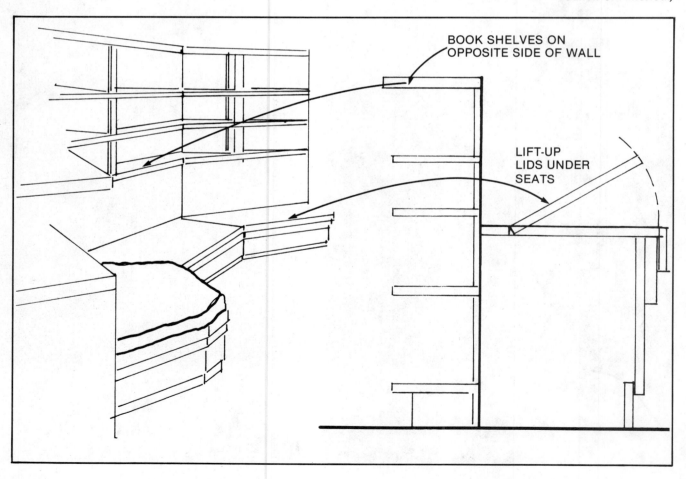

BOOK SHELVES ON OPPOSITE SIDE OF WALL

LIFT-UP LIDS UNDER SEATS

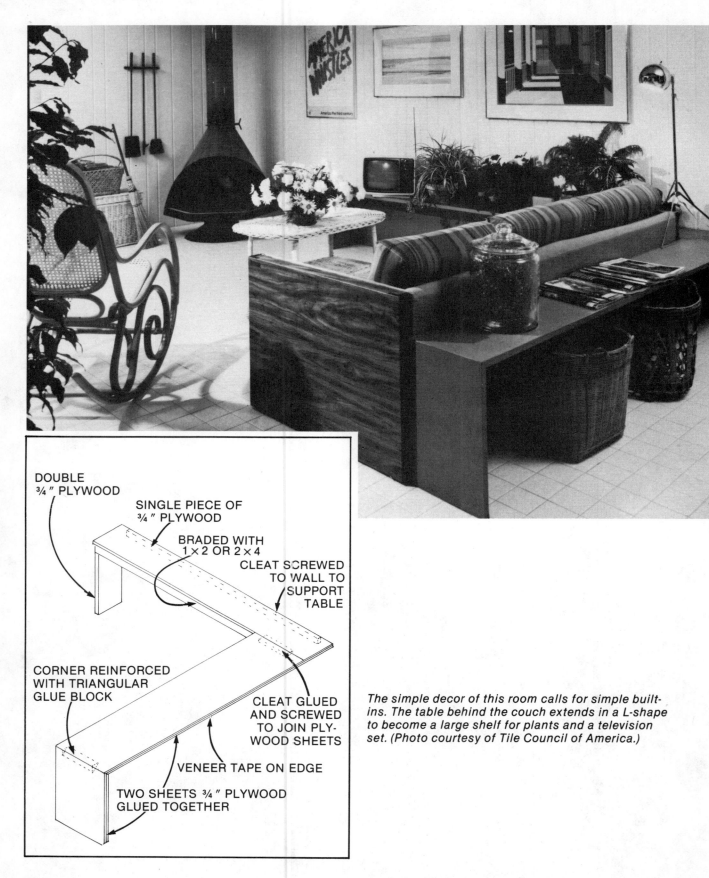

DOUBLE
¾" PLYWOOD

SINGLE PIECE OF
¾" PLYWOOD

BRADED WITH
1 × 2 OR 2 × 4

CLEAT SCREWED
TO WALL TO
SUPPORT
TABLE

CORNER REINFORCED
WITH TRIANGULAR
GLUE BLOCK

CLEAT GLUED
AND SCREWED
TO JOIN PLY-
WOOD SHEETS

VENEER TAPE ON EDGE

TWO SHEETS ¾" PLYWOOD
GLUED TOGETHER

The simple decor of this room calls for simple built-ins. The table behind the couch extends in a L-shape to become a large shelf for plants and a television set. (Photo courtesy of Tile Council of America.)

This simple book shelf built against a living room wall—in a niche—can be ordinary pine shelving of 1 × 6, 1 × 8, 1 × 10 or 1 × 12 stock. For shelves of added thickness, without great increase in weight, shelves can be assembled from framing of 1 × 2s with 1/8- or 1/4-inch hardboard glued and bradded to both sides. Shelves are painted to match the wall. Note that the bottom shelf on each end of the bookcase is flush with top of table at end of sofa. The center section of bookcase is raised to create "frame" for sofa, and provides display of photographs and paintings.

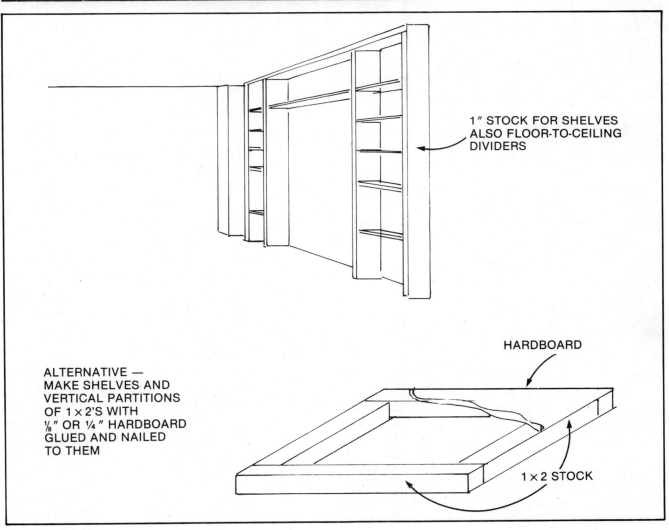

1″ STOCK FOR SHELVES ALSO FLOOR-TO-CEILING DIVIDERS

HARDBOARD

ALTERNATIVE — MAKE SHELVES AND VERTICAL PARTITIONS OF 1 × 2'S WITH ⅛″ OR ¼″ HARDBOARD GLUED AND NAILED TO THEM

1 × 2 STOCK

Dressing Up a Bookshelf

Perhaps in your living room you like comfort mixed with cactus and Columbian artifacts. A combination of wallcoverings might be to your taste, and a built-in corner cabinet could be partly covered with some of the wallcovering. Note the use of molding to separate the upper and lower parts of the walls, and to frame the cabinet doors and drawer front. This room is comfortable and casual, but still has an exciting feel about it.

There are touches of the desert, tropics and ancient civilizations in this comfortable living room. The corner cabinet is a built-in that houses books on shelves; moldings help draw the eye. (Photo courtesy of Wallcovering Industry Bureau, United-DeSoto.)

You can build this impressive bar by applying paneling over a frame, as detailed on pages 50-51.

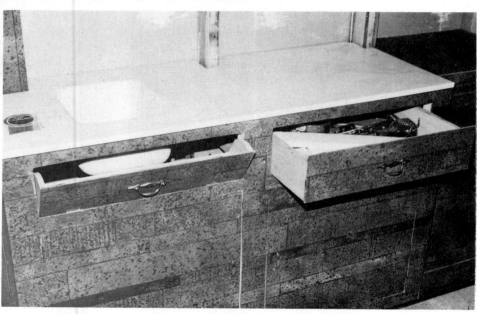

3 Storage Everywhere

STORAGE WALLS

There are literally hundreds of cubic feet of storage space in every home, but that space is completely overlooked—inside interior walls and partitions. Such storage is only a few inches deep, but it is absolutely ideal for such items as canned goods, bottled products, and paper towels.

Some kitchens will have wall space that can be utilized for storing food, and very often the walls of a stairway provide another out-of-the-way location for a wall pantry.

In the example shown, a hallway was converted to a storage area, after the owners decided to panel the walls; this was to be the initial step in creating a "pantry."

First, cover the floor with several layers of newspaper to protect it from falling plaster. Next, hammer a few holes in the wall . . . being careful not to bash any pipes or wires. If there is baseboard molding at the floor, remove it.

Use a level to mark a horizontal line on the wall (or walls) about 5 inches below the ceiling. Score across this line with a linoleum or utility knife. This will be the top of your wall pantry; the ends of the line should be just inside the two studs that will be the ends of your pantry. Set the level vertical, after you have knocked holes in the wall to determine the position of the top and bottom of each end stud, and mark along the wall to indicate where the studs are. Score along the two vertical lines, then break out all the plaster or plasterboard between the two vertical and the horizontal lines, down to the floor. You now have a series of exposed 2 × 4 studs, the backs of which are covered with the plasterboard on the opposite side. If you find wires or pipes, put up a box around them. You don't want canned goods abrading the insulation on wiring, nor banging on pipe connections to cause possible leaks.

A paneled hallway actually is a "pantry" with shelves for canned goods, paper towels, detergent containers, etc., that required dozens of shelves. Except for hinges, there is no sign of "hidden" cabinets.

After plasterboard is removed, you may find wiring or plumbing that will have to be boxed in to protect it. The large mass shown is a plaster-soaked excelsior to hold fixture in bathroom on opposite side of wall.

45

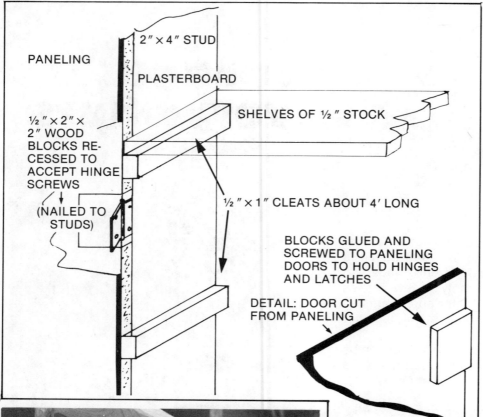

PANELING

2" × 4" STUD

PLASTERBOARD

SHELVES OF ½" STOCK

½" × 2" × 2" WOOD BLOCKS RECESSED TO ACCEPT HINGE SCREWS

(NAILED TO STUDS)

½" × 1" CLEATS ABOUT 4' LONG

BLOCKS GLUED AND SCREWED TO PANELING DOORS TO HOLD HINGES AND LATCHES

DETAIL: DOOR CUT FROM PANELING

Shelf cleats are cut from 1/2-inch stock, and glued and nailed to 2 × 4 studs in wall. Shelves are left loose so they can be removed for storage of items that are quite tall.

Because paneling is only 1/4 inch thick, blocks of 1/2-inch stock are glued and bradded to inside of panel doors to hold hinge screws and attach latch part of touch-type latches.

Shelves are spaced by actually setting various sizes of food tins on each one, then spacing next shelf about 1/4 inch higher for clearance. Here shelves are spaced for small and large food tins, and also for 1-pound coffee cans.

Next, measure the thickness of the plasterboard and shim out the face of each stud by that thickness. Interior plasterboard generally is 3/8 inch, but could be 1/2 inch. Old-fashioned plaster can vary considerably. The ideal is to make each open stud flush with the surface of the wall you have opened.

Measure from the back of each stud opening to the face of the shims. This length will probably be somewhere around 4 inches. Cut cleats of light material, say 1/2 × 1 inch. The spacing of the cleats, and shelves, will depend on the sizes of the items stored. Start from the floor and set packages or cans in place, then space the next shelf up to allow about 1/4 inch above the first row of items. Glue and nail the cleats.

Shelves can be 1/2-inch stock, or plywood that thickness. Don't fasten the shelves, but simply slip them onto the cleats. This makes it possible to remove a shelf when taller items are to be stored on a shelf.

After the shelves and cleats have been positioned, remove the shelves so you can paint the inside

Now you see it . . .

Door for cassette cabinet overlaps opening a couple of inches all around. The inside was painted bright red with a gloss paint.

. . . now you don't!

Small door is cut in wall opposite "pantry" to hold cassette tapes. Hinges used here are the plastic type without pins. Hinges later were painted to match paneling so they were less noticeable.

of the "pantry," painting the back of the plasterboard, the 2 × 4 studs, and the shelves. The next step is the paneling.

Apply the paneling with panel adhesive from a caulking gun. Cartridges of the adhesive are sold in most hardware stores and home centers. A nail gun helps speed the job, and there now are electric-powered nail guns on the market. They speed the job even more, and eliminate the fatigue that used to result from the manual nail guns with their heavy springs.

Cut the paneling right at the beginning of the "pantry" and at the end. In between, cut the doors so they have their edges on 2 × 4's, and the tops and bottoms are on the center line of shelves. Note that it was necessary to glue and screw blocks to the insides of the doors to accept the hinge and latch screws. Blocks also are recessed into the plaster at the end studs. Touch-type latches were used, requiring only a push on the door to open and close it. All that is visible on the "pantry" wall are the backs of the hinges, which can be touched with a matching paint so they

Near right: Wall with cassette cabinet also had broom closet, light switch and thermostat. Trim around door has been removed here. The next step was to cut floor of cabinet flush with surface of plasterboard. Base molding here also was removed before paneling was applied. Far right: After paneling was applied, light-switch cover and thermostat removed and replaced, the closet door is almost invisible. Note that only base shoe (quarter-round) was reapplied, but base molding was not replaced.

blend in with the paneling and are hidden.

Only one wall of the hall shown was used as a pantry; on the opposite wall a small cabinet was made to store tape cassettes. On the same wall there was a broom closet. To conceal the closet, the trim was removed from around the door and the paneling was run to the edges of the opening. The door then was covered with paneling and the door seemed to just disappear.

To finish the job shown, the shoe molding (quarter-round) was replaced but not the

baseboard. This was a decision by the homeowner, and another builder of the wall pantry might prefer to use new molding, of the type sold to match the paneling.

STAIRWAY STORAGE

Stairways are another place where there is storage that often is overlooked. Too often when a basement is remodeled for living space, the stairs are simply painted or carpeted and considered only as a way to get up and down.

An open stairway with treads but no risers is typical of many basements. Steel beam alongside stairway will have to be enclosed with framework, then covered with paneling or plasterboard.

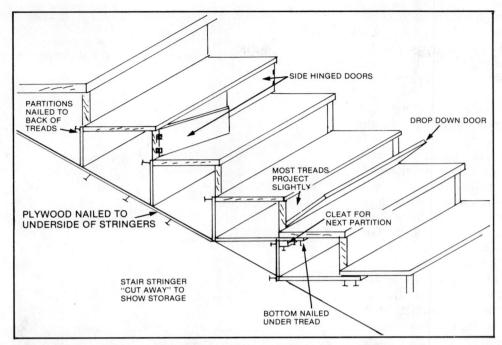

SIDE HINGED DOORS

PARTITIONS NAILED TO BACK OF TREADS

DROP DOWN DOOR

MOST TREADS PROJECT SLIGHTLY

PLYWOOD NAILED TO UNDERSIDE OF STRINGERS

CLEAT FOR NEXT PARTITION

STAIR STRINGER "CUT AWAY" TO SHOW STORAGE

BOTTOM NAILED UNDER TREAD

Open risers of stairway can be made into doors that permit reaching into one of two types of small cabinets built under stairs. One type is created by nailing a sheet of plywood to underside of stringers, then nailing vertical partitions to back edges of treads. You actually would install partitions first, determining their size by holding straightedge across underside of stringers. The second type is made by nailing one piece under tread, and a second piece on back edge of tread. Additional vertical pieces would require 1 × 1-inch cleat as indicated.

Step cabinets could be combined with a closet built under the stairway using shelves and/or clothespole. Shorter space near lower end of stairway could be used for drawers; some could have odd-shape fronts to match angle of steps.

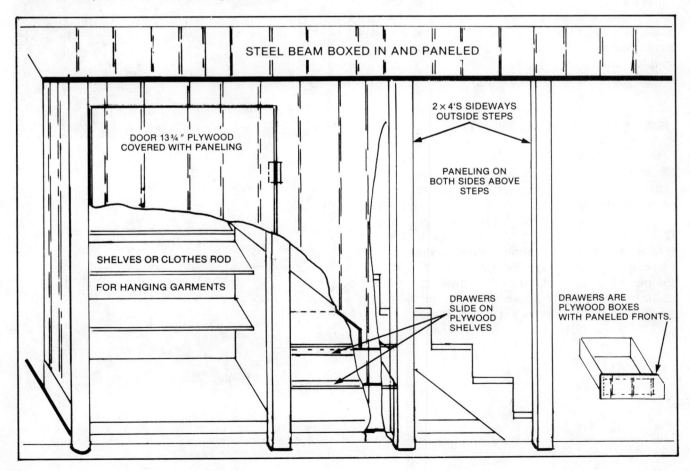

STEEL BEAM BOXED IN AND PANELED

DOOR 13¾" PLYWOOD COVERED WITH PANELING

2 × 4'S SIDEWAYS OUTSIDE STEPS

PANELING ON BOTH SIDES ABOVE STEPS

SHELVES OR CLOTHES ROD

FOR HANGING GARMENTS

DRAWERS SLIDE ON PLYWOOD SHELVES

DRAWERS ARE PLYWOOD BOXES WITH PANELED FRONTS.

Many basement stairs are simple wooden structures consisting of stringers with treads, but no risers. But if you do intend to install risers on this type of stairway, why not make them small doors that open to a series of small but handy cabinets?

Shelves to create the bottoms of the small cabinets can be glued and nailed to the underside of the next lower tread, then boxed-in on the sides and back.

A bit more complicated is the arrangement where vertical "dividers" are nailed to the back edges of the treads; each divider is of a length that brings it flush with the edges of the stringer. A sheet of plywood is nailed to the back edges of the risers to create a series of "boxes" with slanting bottoms. You might want to cut the bottom edges of the dividers at an angle to make them fit snugly against the plywood backing. With a bit of measuring you could determine where to nail through the plywood into the lower edges of the dividers. Drop-down doors would be most practical, but side-hinged doors also could be utilized.

The space under the stairs is another potential storage area, and it is much more apparent in most cases. You could combine the step cabinets with such a closet. Depending on the space available, the under-stair closet could even be a small bar.* When not in use, it could be closed and locked.

USING PANELING FOR CABINETS

If you are building cabinets in a room that is to be paneled, use the paneling as a construction material. A simple framing of 2 × 4s can be used to support the lightweight paneling, and doors can be made by making frames of 1 × 2 stock. Drawers are framed of lighter stock inside the heavier framing, and simple guides assure easy working of the drawers. For an absolute match of the paneling, cut a piece to fit completely over the cabinet framing, then make cutouts for the doors and drawers. The saw kerfs provide necessary clearance for both the doors. and drawers.

This impressive bar is a framing of 2 × 4s covered with the same paneling used for the walls. Paneling also covers the exposed studs in the wall and is cut into shallow arches for above the bar.

Here one piece of paneling is cut to fit face of cabinet, then cut-outs made for doors and drawers. Even if some cuts are a bit irregular, the cut-outs match the openings exactly.

For instructions on how to build a bar, see Chapter 5 of Successful Living Rooms.

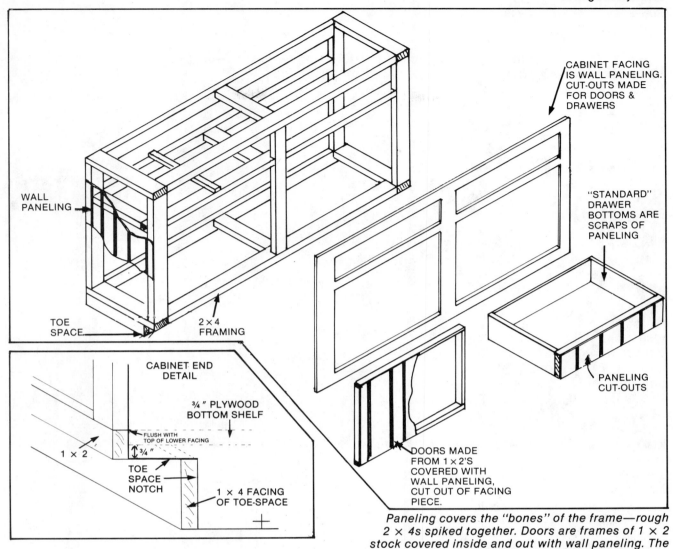

WALL
PANELING

TOE
SPACE

2 × 4
FRAMING

CABINET FACING
IS WALL PANELING.
CUT-OUTS MADE
FOR DOORS &
DRAWERS

"STANDARD"
DRAWER
BOTTOMS ARE
SCRAPS OF
PANELING

PANELING
CUT-OUTS

DOORS MADE
FROM 1 × 2'S
COVERED WITH
WALL PANELING,
CUT OUT OF FACING
PIECE.

CABINET END
DETAIL

¾" PLYWOOD
BOTTOM SHELF

FLUSH WITH
TOP OF LOWER FACING

¾"

1 × 2

TOE
SPACE
NOTCH

1 × 4 FACING
OF TOE-SPACE

Paneling covers the "bones" of the frame—rough 2 × 4s spiked together. Doors are frames of 1 × 2 stock covered inside and out with wall paneling. The front of the cabinet is one piece of paneling with cut-outs made for doors and drawers.

STORAGE COUCH

For the rustic look of wood in your living room, try embossed hardboard wall paneling. It is not only great for walls, whether applied vertically or diagonally, but can also be applied to any built-in that is constructed of solid lumber framing.

Like so many built-ins, the couch is basically a box made by spiking together 2 × 4s for the main frame, then covering it with wall paneling. The "seat" of the couch is sheets of plywood that can be hinged to expose "hidden" storage beneath. Foam-rubber cushions, or a foam-rubber mattress get covers of upholstery material, and the couch doubles as extra sleeping space on occasion. An added touch is a shelf around the top of the couch covered with ceramic tile. The shelf is a convenient place for cups of coffee or glasses of beverage, and it cleans easily with a damp cloth. So you have a couch, counter and storage cabinet in one.

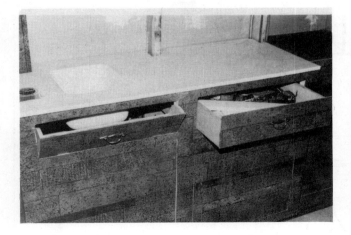

Doors are assembled from 1 × 2 and covered with paneling, hung with plain butt hinges. Matching hardware used on drawers is bolted through fronts. Note that "drawer" in front of sink actually is tilt-down bin.

Wallpaper, matching fabric and molding are combined in this corner built-in that creates a cheerful seating area, ample storage in compartments below. (Photo courtesy of Wallcovering Industry Bureau, Christopher Prints.)

SEAT BACK

STORAGE UNDER SEAT (CUSHIONS REMOVED)

END VIEW

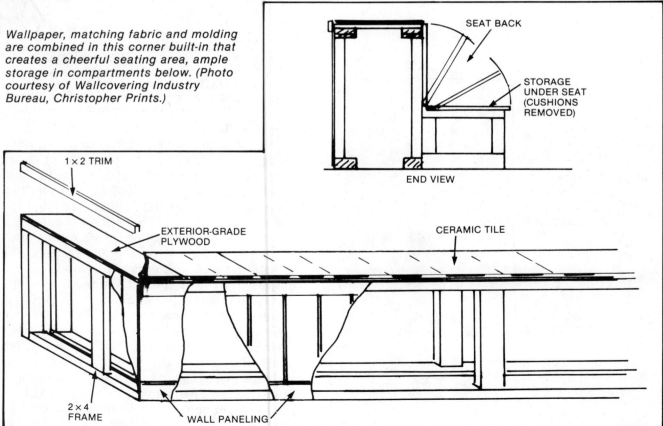

1 × 2 TRIM

EXTERIOR-GRADE PLYWOOD

CERAMIC TILE

2 × 4 FRAME

WALL PANELING

"Secret" panels are actually doors cut from plywood, trimmed with molding, inside of which wallcovering material is applied. Floor space is obtained by building wall out from original wall alongside fireplace. (Photo courtesy of Western Wood Moulding and Millwork Producers.)

FIREPLACE FOOTAGE

If you are going to do a remodeling job in a living room, family room or basement, you can create secret panels and provide storage for all kinds of items by building a "giant" cabinet from floor to ceiling. It need be only a few inches deep, or as deep as you wish. Where there is a fireplace that extends into the room, the cabinet can be built flush with the face of the fireplace surround, or perhaps a few inches back of it.

In the photo examples shown, plywood has been used for the cabinet, and the doors are simply pieces of the same 3/4-inch plywood. Each door has been trimmed with molding and wallpaper, or a wallcovering material applied inside the molding. To make the cabinets really "secret," similar molded panels are located on other walls in the room.

In the room shown the decor is colonial, and the lower portions of the walls have a "wainscoting" of paneling that is painted. The same kind of secret doors are installed in the wainscoting. Shallow cabinets could be created, similar to the "wall pantry" on regular walls, using the molded-panel door idea.

There is a wide variety of stock moldings available, and you may combine several molding shapes to create your own individual molding. The molding should not be too heavy in a small room; conversely, very thin or light weight molding would look out of place in a larger room.

Touch-type latches would be ideal for the doors over the secret compartments, but some provision should be made to minimize finger and hand prints. You might consider a coat of clear flat varnish to prevent the paint from being smudged. The varnish also would make it easy to wipe away any marks that were made.

Panels on new wall match those on exterior wall, but there are no "secret" cabinets behind panels on outside wall. (Photo courtesy of Western Wood Moulding and Millwork Producers.)

Close-up of cabinets with doors open show that they are simply plywood boxes. Metal brackets are fitted on cabinet sides to permit adjusting shelves to any height desired. There also are "secret" panels on lower part of wall below chair rail. These smaller doors are trimmed with molding, but are painted rather than papered. (Photo courtesy of Western Wood Moulding and Millwork Producers.)

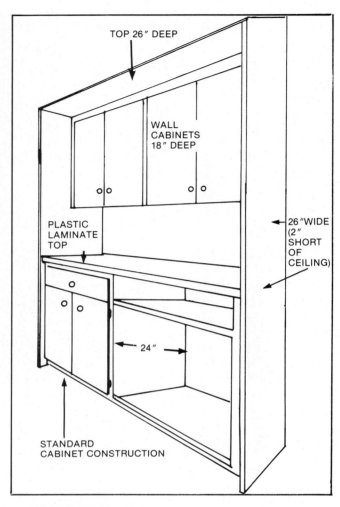

In large kitchen, one end can be partitioned off with room divider that runs almost floor to ceiling. Ironing board can be hidden behind it; generous cabinets and drawers provide storage; counter is used for folding clothes and for other tasks. The room divider is basically a large free-standing base and wall cabinet such as built in a kitchen. Sides and top of divider are 2 inches wider than cabinet, so cabinet is not readily visible from sides.

Diagram labels: TOP 26" DEEP · WALL CABINETS 18" DEEP · PLASTIC LAMINATE TOP · 26" WIDE (2" SHORT OF CEILING) · 24" · STANDARD CABINET CONSTRUCTION

CORNER CABINETS

Ready-made corner cabinets are easy-to-install built-ins. Finished or unfinished cabinets of this type are not too expensive and require no real carpentry work. They simply are fitted into a corner; it might be necessary to notch the back edges of the cabinet to fit over existing molding. Also note, shown in the same room with the corner cabinet, a shelf on two walls up near the ceiling that provides storage and displays prized china and other items. The underside of the shelf is fitted with hooks to hang some prized mugs.

Molding supports this shelf along the wall, being nailed to the studs. Further support is provided by wooden brackets nailed on either side of the window trim, and to the studs at convenient locations. The railing is assembled from ready-made wooden spindles that are fitted in holes spaced equidistant in the top surface of the shelf, and in spaced holes in a 3/4 × 3/4-inch strip that is the top rail of the gallery.

Ready-made corner cabinet creates handy "built-in," but can be taken with you to another home. Shelf on wall up near ceiling must remain, but is a handy and unusual "built-in" (Photo courtesy of Western Wood Moulding and Millwork Producers.)

In basement sewing room mirrors are attached to hinged plywood panels so they can close face-to-face, and only the wall panels show. Drop-down table is 3/4-inch plywood, trimmed with molding, covered with wall paneling. (Photo courtesy of Masonite Corporation.)

SEWING CRANNIES

Don't overlook the sewing machine when you are remodeling either upstairs, in the attic, or in the basement. There should be a place on one of these three levels for a really first-class sewing room.

Cabinets should be floor-to-ceiling, carried out with the same steps as for the storage wall discussed early in the chapter. Bi-fold doors will make the sewing machine and cutting table readily accessible, yet completely hidden when not in use. An added touch is a three-panel mirror that is just great when fitting and adjusting garments. In the arrangement shown, the two smaller side mirrors close on the larger one to completely disappear. The backs of the pivoting mirrors are covered with paneling to match the rest of the walls.

BONUS SURFACES

If you build a handy work surface that can be used for hobbies and games, make it an inch or two higher off the floor and then build tables that slide under it. When there is a group or party in the house, the extra tables will really be useful. When not needed, they slide under the work counter and are completely out of the way.

Finally, be aware that most closets are extremely inefficient. You usually have one hanger rod or pole about 5 feet off the floor, with perhaps a shelf above you can barely reach. There may be space on the floor for shoes and odds and ends, but never enough. Investigate the modern hardware, shelving and devices now available that can really organize a closet, whether it's for an adult or child. Check hardware stores or home centers for these products.

A simple stunt like making your work counter a couple of inches higher than usual allows storage of spare table under it — a bonus also for extra guests and for parties.

Ready-made units are handy even for youngsters, helping them to put away their clothes neatly; mother has handy and practical storage above. (Photo courtesy of Kinkead Industries.)

"Colonial" look was given these cabinets by using stain of "early-American" color, and addition of simple wooden knobs rather than metal pulls. (Photo courtesy of Armstrong Cork Co.) ▶

*Flush doors in these kitchen cabinets have arched openings with cloth inserts supported by metal grille. Rabbet on back side of opening permits securing of both cloth and grille.
(Photo courtesy of Armstrong Cork Co.)*

*The modern look of these cabinets was created with a stenciled pattern that duplicates the painted design on each door. Note how the design is repeated in adjacent room with wallcovering and hanging acrylic-plastic decorator piece.
(Photo courtesy of Armstrong Cork Co.)*

These cabinets were painted with a ground coat, then an antique glaze was used to create the "grained" look. (Photo courtesy of Armstrong Cork Co.)

Painted cabinets in this kitchen have flush doors and drawer fronts to present a smooth surface. (Photo courtesy of Armstrong Cork Co.)

"Wild side" of birch plywood was used for these cabinets so they have strong character, as opposed to grainless good side of birch normally used. (Photo courtesy of Armstrong Cork Co.)

An outdated bathroom presents a real decorating challenge. (Photo courtesy of Aster Products)

4 Bathroom Cabinets & Vanities

Bathroom cabinets are similar to those used in kitchens; the cabinets differ mostly in what they store. Rather than dishes and food, towels, washcloths, soap and other bathroom needs are handled.

Because a bathroom is somewhat smaller than a kitchen, it takes less time and money to remodel it. Which means that you can "let yourself go" with the cabinets and the wallcovering to create a truly luxurious area.

The various photos show a number of different decorating schemes, but all are basically vanity cabinets (the base cabinet that contains the wash basin), plus floor- and wall-coverings that are water-resistant and beautiful.

We will describe one bathroom remodeling (see bottom photo on page 60) with period-design cabinets, elegant wall paneling and pastel fixtures. The wall paneling shown is real wood: 3/8-inch planking that is given a waterproof coating of sealer that retains the natural color and look of the wood. Check at your paint or hardware store for this sealer; it is the type used to waterproof wood used outdoors such as wood decks.

This bathroom has carpeted floor, vanity cabinet has two basins. Cabinet is painted, with drawers a darker color than doors. Doors have touch-type latches, drawers are opened by pulling on top edge of front. This style drawer is not recommended for bathroom where children are apt to leave hand and fingerprints. (Photo courtesy of Armstrong Cork Co.)

This attic room has skylight, all-over pattern of wallcovering on cabinet doors and room door. Drawers are not shown in the cabinet, but pull-out bins behind doors would be substitute. (Photo courtesy of Wallcovering Information Bureau)

Good-sized knobs are used as pulls on the doors and drawers of this cabinet located in a bathroom used by two boys. "Flexalum" chrome aluminum blind divides the two areas, yet provides light and air along with privacy. (Photo courtesy of Flexalum Decor Blinds)

Bathrooms vary so much in size and shape that it is highly unlikely that you will duplicate the arrangement shown. You can follow guidelines, however, as they apply to your particular room.

FIRST STEPS

Floor Plan

The first step in the remodeling is to make a floor plan to scale. Because a bathroom generally is a smallish room, use a larger scale than the generally used 1/4-inch-to-the-foot. Instead, go to 1/2, 3/4 or 1 inch to the foot. The larger size makes planning easier.

Your drawing should show the location of the existing fixtures and their sizes. Draw in the cabinets you want to build and/or install. Try to keep the vanity basin in about the same position as the present one to avoid unnecessary additional plumbing. This is not a hard-and-fast rule, however, as you can extend the existing piping with adapters to flexible polybutylene (PB) plastic piping that can be snaked through walls and under cabinets much like electrical wiring.

Fixtures

If the walls are to be paneled, the existing water-closet tank (if it is fastened to the wall) and the lavatory basin must be disconnected and removed. If there are no shut-off valves in the lines to the lavatory basin and the toilet, now is the time to install them. Later, if you need to do any repairing to the faucets or plumbing, you can shut off just one fixture rather than shutting off water to the whole house.

Walls

If adding paneling, walls must be reasonably smooth and flat. If this is the case and the plaster or plasterboard is firmly attached to the studs, you can apply any kind of paneling with panel adhesive. Before using the adhesive, remove dirt, loose paint or wallpaper with a wirebrush or dull putty knife.

Where walls are uneven or the plaster is loose, you will need furring strips to which the paneling can be attached. Space the strips about 16 inches on center (or as detailed in the instructions with the paneling), and nail them to the wall studs. The

If walls are flat and smooth, plasterboard firmly attached, paneling can be applied with adhesive. All dirt, loose paint or paper must first be removed when adhesive is used.

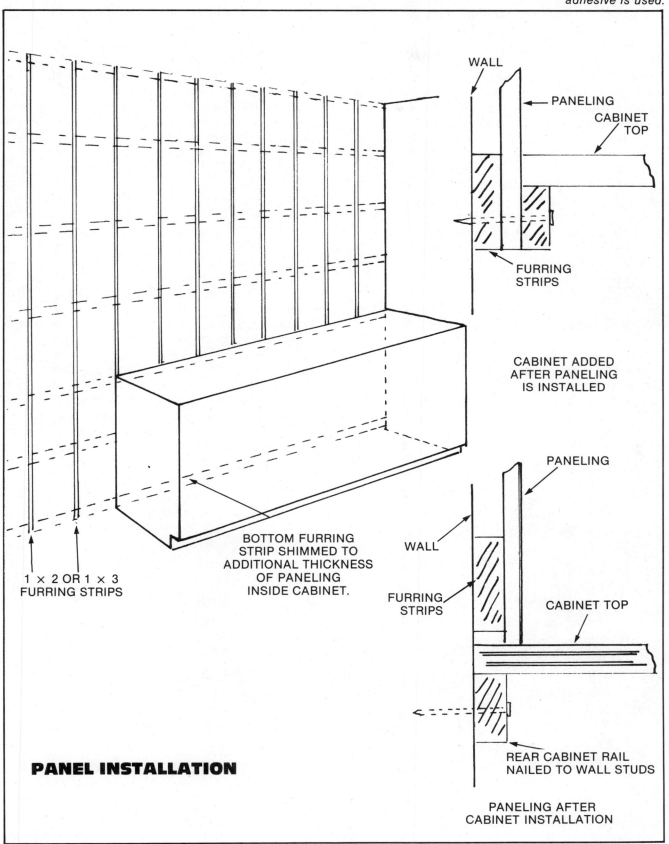

WALL

PANELING

CABINET TOP

FURRING STRIPS

CABINET ADDED
AFTER PANELING
IS INSTALLED

PANELING

WALL

FURRING STRIPS

CABINET TOP

REAR CABINET RAIL
NAILED TO WALL STUDS

PANELING AFTER
CABINET INSTALLATION

1 × 2 OR 1 × 3
FURRING STRIPS

BOTTOM FURRING
STRIP SHIMMED TO
ADDITIONAL THICKNESS
OF PANELING
INSIDE CABINET.

PANEL INSTALLATION

strips can be spaced vertically, directly over the studs, or horizontally across them. Sometimes the horizontal strips are spaced more than 16 inches, depending on the panel-maker's instructions, so be sure to follow them. Keep the furring strips in a flat, vertical plane by placing shims under low spots, and holding the shims with nails driven through the furring strips.

The wall behind a cabinet need not be paneled because the existing wall can serve as the panel back. In this case, let the paneling run down about 2 inches below the top of the base cabinet, and behind any exposed ends of a cabinet. Where furring is required under the paneling, use the arrangement in Detail A, where the cabinet is installed after the paneling is finished. If the cabinet already is in place, run the paneling down to the top of the cabinet as in Detail B.

VANITY CABINET

It is absolutely necessary that the vanity cabinet be level, so shim up the floor at low spots so the bottom rails of the cabinet are firmly supported at points no more than 24 inches apart. The shims should not, of course, project beyond the cabinet base, so first mark on the floor the exact location of the cabinet, then use a level and straightedge to locate the necessary shims.

To build a vanity cabinet like the one shown on page 65, follow the detailed drawing. The ends and partitions can be edge-glued solid stock or plywood. Partitions are identical, but the end panel is different. The horizontal piece at the lower front rail that provides a toe space is rabbeted at the back edge to accept the bottom of the cabinet. Notches are cut at the front for the upright members. Assemble the end panel and partitions with the bottom rear and front rails, along with the top rear rail, then set the cabinet in position. Nail the back rails to the wall studs or furring strips. If one end of the cabinet joins an adjacent wall, use cleats to support the cabinet top and bottom instead of a panel. Cleats are nailed to the partitions and end panel to support the bottom, which is cut next. Nail on the front frame. The vertical members of the frame cover the edges of the partitions and are centered over them.

Make cutouts in the wide, top front rails to form drawer openings, then nail the end vertical pieces to this rail. Use cleats to support the drawer slides. Cleats on partitions and at cabinet ends are of different thicknesses so they will be flush with the ends of the drawer cutouts.

If you have restricted space in your bathroom, it may be necessary to reduce the width of the vanity cabinet a bit. In this case, however, be sure there is enough room between the basin and the

Vanity cabinet must be level, so check floor with aid of straightedge piece of lumber, 24 or 36-inch level. Note low spots, mark them for placement of shingle shims. (Photo courtesy of Western Wood Products Association)

Mark location of cabinet on floor, then tack shims to floor, positioning them so they do not project beyond cabinet, are hidden in final installation. (Photo courtesy of Western Wood Products Association)

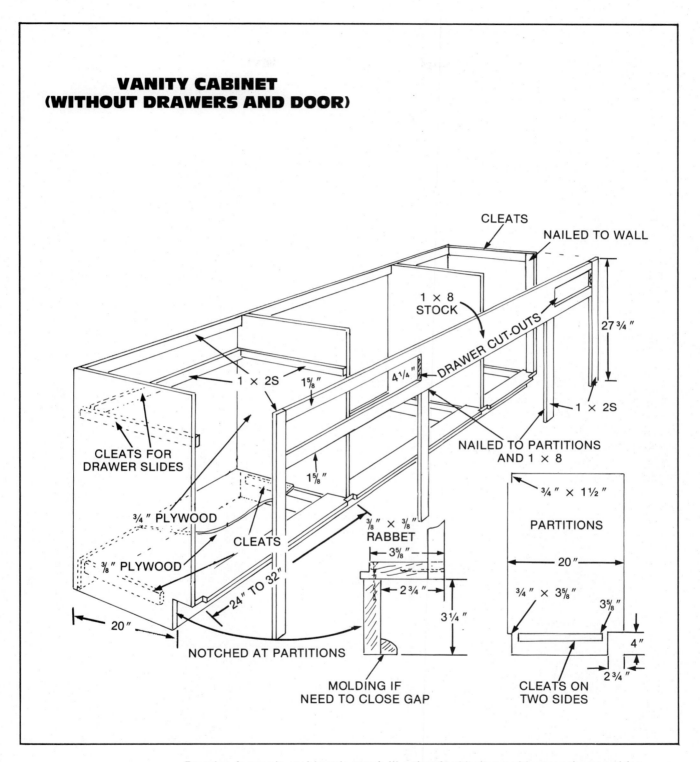

VANITY CABINET
(WITHOUT DRAWERS AND DOOR)

CLEATS

NAILED TO WALL

1 × 8
STOCK

DRAWER CUT-OUTS

27¾"

4¼"

1 × 2S

1 × 2S

1⅝"

NAILED TO PARTITIONS
AND 1 × 8

CLEATS FOR
DRAWER SLIDES

1⅝"

¾" PLYWOOD

CLEATS

¾" × 1½"

PARTITIONS

20"

⅜" PLYWOOD

⅜" × ⅜"
RABBET

3⅝"

2¾"

3¼"

¾" × 3⅝"

3⅝"

4"

24" TO 32"

20"

NOTCHED AT PARTITIONS

MOLDING IF
NEED TO CLOSE GAP

CLEATS ON
TWO SIDES

2¾"

Framing for vanity cabinet is much like that for kitchen cabinets, other used for storage. Main difference is top with provision for basins.

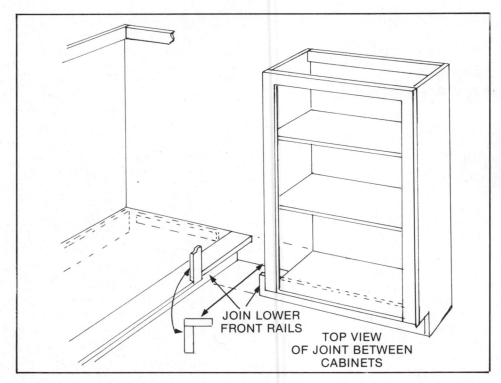

Narrow Cabinet Between Vanity & Stool (Without Top & Door)

JOIN LOWER FRONT RAILS

TOP VIEW OF JOINT BETWEEN CABINETS

Basin Installation

Vanity basins come in two main types, those that fasten to top of counter, are held with stainless-steel ring and clamps. Other type is attached to underside of vanity top, held with screws and brackets.

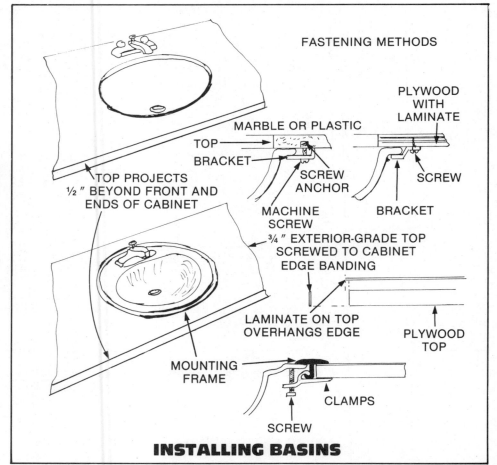

FASTENING METHODS

PLYWOOD WITH LAMINATE

MARBLE OR PLASTIC

TOP

BRACKET

SCREW ANCHOR

MACHINE SCREW

SCREW

BRACKET

TOP PROJECTS ½ " BEYOND FRONT AND ENDS OF CABINET

¾ " EXTERIOR-GRADE TOP SCREWED TO CABINET EDGE BANDING

LAMINATE ON TOP OVERHANGS EDGE

PLYWOOD TOP

MOUNTING FRAME

CLAMPS

SCREW

INSTALLING BASINS

back rail for the faucet. There are several sizes of round and oval basins, which permits some flexibility in their position in the countertop.

Countertop

If your woodworking skills are a bit limited, or your workshop space is not adequate, you can get a cabinetmaker to cut a countertop to size and to cover it with plastic laminate in your choice of color and pattern. If you want to handle the project yourself, use 3/4-inch plywood and cut it so it extends 1/2 inch beyond the front and exposed ends of the cabinet. Add a filler strip as detailed. Fasten the top to the cabinet with countersunk flathead screws or use angle brackets underneath. The brackets permit easy removal of the top should that ever be necessary.

Sand the plywood clean and remove sanding dust with a tack cloth. Cut the laminate a bit larger than the top, as described in Chapter 1, where applying laminate to countertops is detailed, and Chapter 9.

Should you choose one of the new decorated vitreous china vanity basins that are attached to the underside of the cabinet top, it's a good idea to have a top of solid plastic or marble cut to the required size, with the basin opening cut in it. Marble tops are drilled for screw anchors with a special carbide-tipped bit.

This kind of basin also can be used in a plywood top covered with plastic laminate. With the plywood top, the underside for a width of about 3 inches around the cutout is covered with fiberglass cloth and an epoxy resin. When this coating is dry, it can be sanded smooth for a good seal against the basin, and it will be waterproof.

Drop-in basins require a stainless-steel clamping ring that is held by special clamps. Calking is applied under the edges that contact the basin and top. Excess calking is wiped away after the ring is pulled down snugly by the clamps.

If you use angle brackets to attach the top, you can install the basin before attaching the top. This makes the job a lot easier, and the brackets also assure that in later years you can readily remove the top to change the basin or replace the laminate if you change the bathroom decor.

In the photo a narrow end cabinet was built between the vanity cabinet and the water closet to utilize every bit of space. A cabinet like this can be installed as detailed, but allowance must be made for the narrow cabinet when building the vanity cabinet. Rather than a partition next to the drawer cutout and the door opening, just a drawer-support strip is installed, so all of the corner space can be utilized. Note that both the cabinet top and flooring extend to the adjacent wall.

The laminate on the tops of the two cabinets is butted tightly together to minimize the joint, or

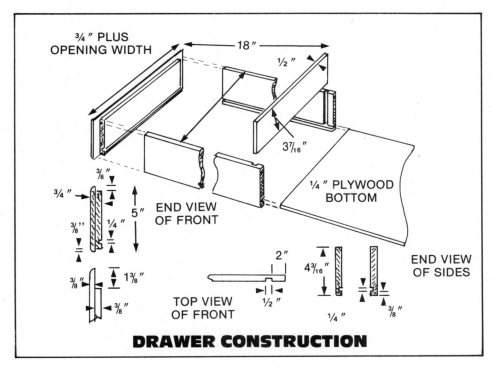

DRAWER CONSTRUCTION

¾″ PLUS OPENING WIDTH · 18″ · ½″ · 3⁷⁄₁₆″ · ¼″ PLYWOOD BOTTOM · END VIEW OF FRONT · 5″ · ¾″ · ⅜″ · ¼″ · 1⅜″ · ⅜″ · TOP VIEW OF FRONT · 2″ · ½″ · 4³⁄₁₆″ · ¼″ · ⅜″ · END VIEW OF SIDES

This drawer is variation on "standard" construction shown in Chapter 1, describing drawers used in kitchen cabinets. Back is fitted in vertical dadoes in sides.

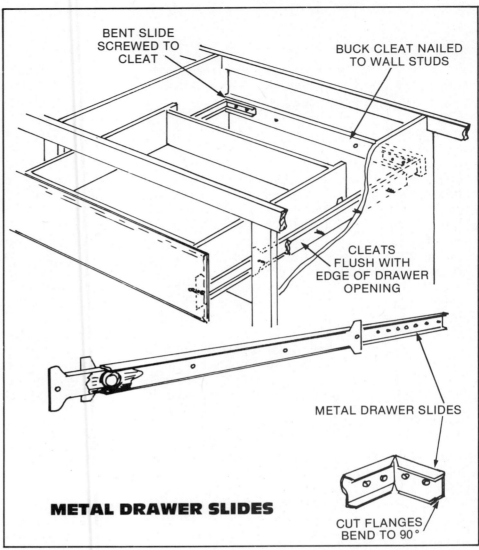

BENT SLIDE
SCREWED TO
CLEAT

BUCK CLEAT NAILED
TO WALL STUDS

For any kind of drawer, ball-bearing slides make operation much easier. Various types are available, so always read instructions packed with them, make drawers a size that provides proper clearance for the devices.

CLEATS
FLUSH WITH
EDGE OF DRAWER
OPENING

METAL DRAWER SLIDES

METAL DRAWER SLIDES

CUT FLANGES
BEND TO 90°

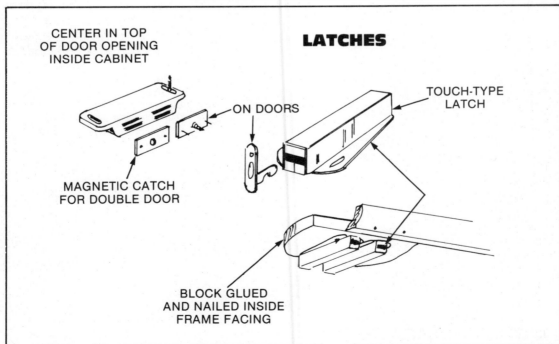

LATCHES

CENTER IN TOP
OF DOOR OPENING
INSIDE CABINET

ON DOORS

TOUCH-TYPE
LATCH

MAGNETIC CATCH
FOR DOUBLE DOOR

The same variety of magnetic and mechanical catches and latches can be used for a vanity cabinet as for kitchen cabinets. Some types of latches are fastened to a shelf, others require a block under the edge of the upper facing strip.

BLOCK GLUED
AND NAILED INSIDE
FRAME FACING

Large mirror in bathroom, especially where there are two basins in vanity, are practical. The mirror also makes the room look bigger, lighter. (Photo courtesy of Tile Council of America)

the top can be cut as an L-shaped piece of plywood with laminate trim already applied to the L-shape. The latter method is more time-consuming and expensive, as there is considerable waste of laminate.

Drawers

Drawings show a variation of the "standard" method of making drawers. In this variation, the back sets on the top of the bottom, but is held in two dadoes cut vertically in the sides.

For easy drawer operation in any kind of cabinet, metal slides with ball-bearing rollers are best. And they do eliminate the need for wooden drawer guides, which simplifies drawer construction.

The metal slides are screwed to the lower edges of the sides of a drawer and to cleats on the cabinet partitions and ends. Slides of this type vary in construction and in details of attachment, but usually are made in lengths that are cut to fit a cabinet. The type shown has flanges that are notched in a V-shape where the bend is made, and the bent ends are screwed to the back of the cabinet, or to a cleat on the wall if there is no back in the cabinet.

Doors

Doors for the bathroom cabinet can be any of the types described and detailed in Chapter 1, as used for kitchen cabinets. Most mechanical door catches require the use of knobs or pulls, but you can eliminate the pulls by using "Tutch-Latches." With this type latch you push on a door to close it,

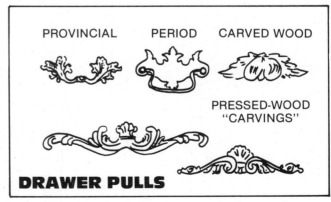

As described in Chapter 1 on kitchen cabinets, choice of pulls and hardware give cabinets their character. Molded-wood carvings provide touch of elegance to these cabinets in bathroom.

push again to open it. This type latch is ideal for doors that are decorated with a wallcovering or cloth. It's a good idea, however, to screw on a square or rectangle of clear plastic where the door will be touched to open or close it. The plastic will protect the decorator material from be-

ing soiled by hands or fingers, and is easily wiped clean.

Period-design pulls, if you wish to use them, are available in antique brass or bronze finishes. You also can get carved-wood pulls if that goes better with your decorating scheme.

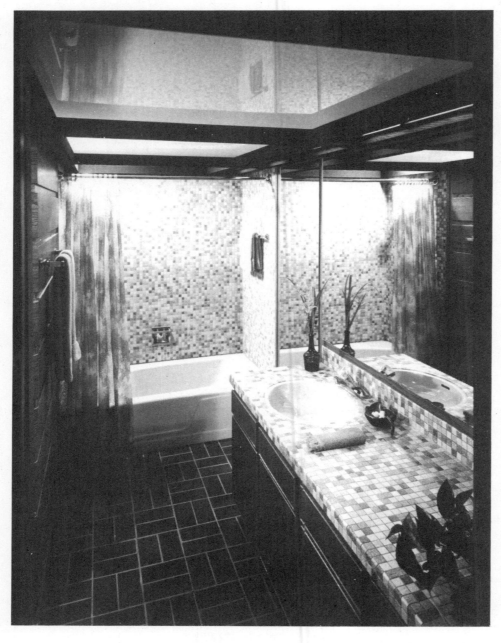

Large mirror in this bathroom runs from top of ceramic-tile vanity to ceiling that consists of framed panels of transluscent plastic with lights above them. (Photo courtesy of Tile Council of America)

5 Bedroom Built-ins & Shelves

BEDS

Built-ins and cabinets are just great for a bedroom, because it generally is one of the smaller rooms in the house (with some few exceptions), yet it has the largest piece of furniture — the bed. Other storage units — dressers and closets — further take up living space.

Which means that the logical first step in planning a remodeling job in a bedroom is to figure a way to minimize the bulk of a bed. You cannot, of course, actually reduce the size of a bed, but by building it in, and making it do service for something other than just a sleeping platform, you can increase the size of the available floor space.

One basic example is to build a bed in a corner of the room, making it a bit higher than "standard." The space underneath then can be used as cabinets with shelves and drawers. This quite possibly could allow you to eliminate a dresser or chest of drawers that is taking up several square feet of floor space.

A built-in bed—it could be called a "bunk", depending on the styling and design—basically is a platform on top of a box to support a mattress. It is possible to use both a box spring and a mattress, but the resulting bed would be quite high. In most cases just a mattress is used; modern units can be obtained in soft, medium and firm, as well as extra-firm types; an inner-spring mattress underneath has little or no effect on the resiliency of the mattress.

One thing to keep in mind when you are designing and constructing a built-in bed is that the bed must be made at frequent intervals. Many housewives find built-in and bunk beds a real problem when it comes to fitting sheets, blankets and pillows on them. Because they are built-in, you cannot walk around them, so you have to work from just one side. This means wrestling with the far side of the mattress to tuck in sheets and blankets, and risking bumped heads and bruised elbows along with strained backs.

Absolutely do not consider placing any built-in bed against the wall if the mattress will be wider than for a single bed, which measures 39 inches wide and 75 inches long. A youth-bed mattress, or an "all-purpose" mattress is even better, as you can buy this type in lengths of 72 inches, and widths of 27, 36 and 39 inches. These mattresses are sold by larger mail-order houses, and some furniture stores.

If you are going to use a new mattress for a built-in, be sure to have it on hand before you start your building. The platform should be just a bit wider and longer than the mattress, especially if there are sides on the platform, as might be necessary for a restless youngster. Remember that the mattress has to be lifted when the bed is made. Any additional straining will just make the bed-maker that much more aggravated.

Be sure to allow space around the mattress for the thickness of a mattress cover, if one is used, plus the two sheets and blankets and the spread. Make sure it's a nice, easy fit, not one that cramps hands and breaks fingernails.

A built-in bed basically is a cabinet, and can be made of 3/4-inch plywood. If the room is paneled, you might want the bed to be of a contrasting hardwood-plywood, or to match the wall paneling. Veneered plywood 3/4 inch thick is a bit expensive, so it makes more sense to build the bed of 3/4 or 5/8-inch fir plywood, to which you brad and glue the same 1/8 or 1/4-inch paneling used on the walls.

A couple of the built-in beds shown have been covered with wallpaper; when this is done you need a smoother surface than plywood. A smooth-surfaced particleboard can be used, and this

Bunk bed built into corner of room has front of ¾-inch plywood, in which openings are cut for drawers and cabinets. Framework underneath can be "standard" lightweight framing with sheet of plywood to support a foam-rubber mattress, or can be a rough frame of 2 × 4 stock. (Photo courtesy of Wallcovering Bureau)

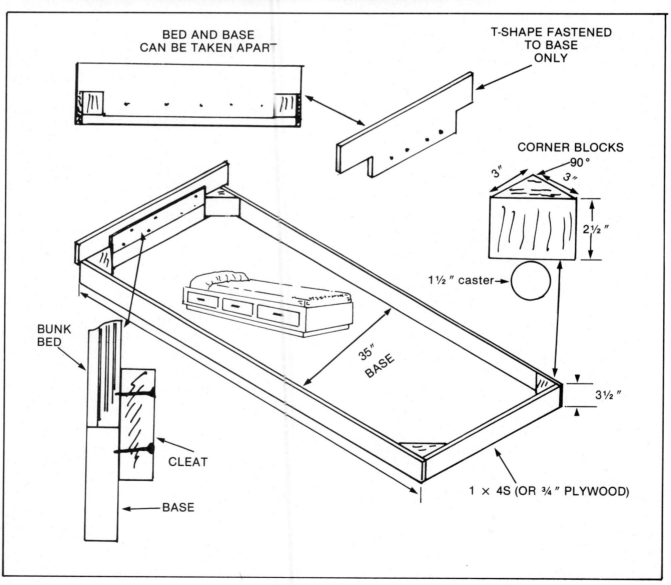

BED AND BASE
CAN BE TAKEN APART

T-SHAPE FASTENED
TO BASE
ONLY

CORNER BLOCKS

3"   90°   3"

2½"

1½" caster

BUNK
BED

CLEAT

35"
BASE

BASE

3½"

1 × 4S (OR ¾" PLYWOOD)

wood-base material comes in a variety of thicknesses. Alternately, use 1/2 or 5/8-inch plywood, to which 1/8 or 1/4-inch hardboard is glued. The smooth side of the hardboard, of course, is faced outward to accept the wallpaper or other wallcovering material.

If a bedroom is located in a converted attic, floor space is an even more critical problem than on the lower floors. On the other hand, a built-in bed can be positioned under the low portion of the slanting ceiling, leaving the higher part of the ceiling for activities that require standing up. Storage can be built under the bed, and at one or both ends.

If space is really a problem, you can even make the bed like an oversize drawer that slides into the

low part of the wall. The bed can move into the wall its full width, if space allows, or it can be designed to project partway to provide daytime seating. The recess into which the bed slides must be made dust-tight so the bed stays clean when it is stored away. A means for ventilation also would be a good idea.

For really simple construction, you can build a rough frame of 2 × 4s to which you glue and brad the wall paneling. You do need a sheet of plywood to support the mattress; the plywood can be as thin as 1/2 inch if you have enough crosspieces to provide adequate support.

If you want to spend some time and money on the bed cabinet, you can build large drawers and install them with heavy-duty ball-bearing slides.

This "standard" lightweight framing for a bunk bed can be made to set in one place on a base, or base can be fitted with spherical casters so bed can be moved. Both long sides have toe space so bed can be turned either way, or used in center of room. Ends are flush with base; bunk and base can be fastened together with strip of wood at each end. Alternately, a T-shape piece of wood is fastened to base inside corner blocks to prevent bunk from moving sideways or end-to-end.

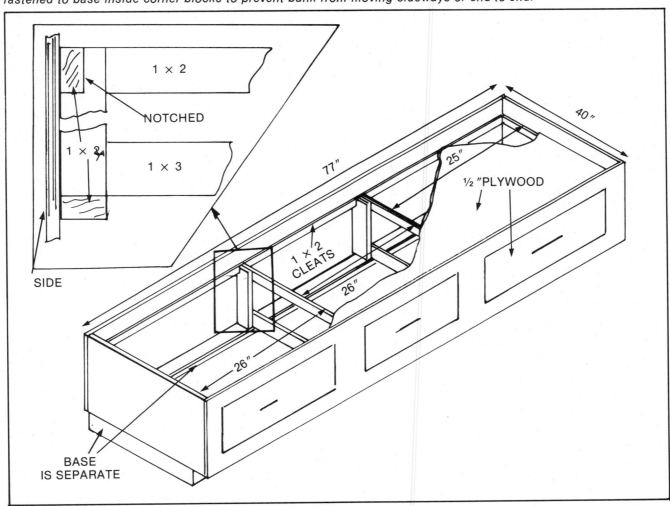

Dramatic bedroom is created in an attic area on step-up platform, with the bed a simple plywood box supported by framing. Note how use of wallcovering makes this a really interesting area. (Photo courtesy of Wallcovering Bureau; "Navajo" pattern by Style-Tex.)

To provide more floor space in children's bedroom, bunks can be built into what was walk-in closet. Simple frame of 2-inch lumber supports sheets of plywood on which mattresses are placed. Facing of bunks is ⅜-inch plywood that comes flush with wallboard that also is ⅜-inch thick. Here wall-covering is applied right over bunk facings. (Photo courtesy of Wallcovering Bureau; "Meadowland" wallcovering by Style-Tex)

Structure of bunk is framed much like wall assembly, with 2 × 4 and 2 × 6 lumber. It would not be too difficult to install drawers under both top and bottom bunks; framing of 1 × 2s would be sufficient.

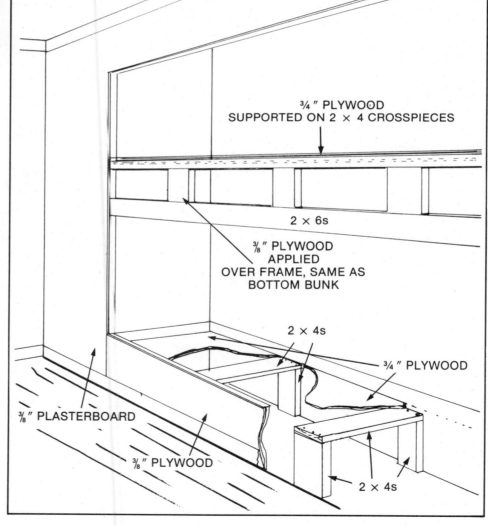

¾" PLYWOOD
SUPPORTED ON 2 × 4 CROSSPIECES

2 × 6s

⅜" PLYWOOD
APPLIED
OVER FRAME, SAME AS
BOTTOM BUNK

2 × 4s

¾" PLYWOOD

⅜" PLASTERBOARD

⅜" PLYWOOD

2 × 4s

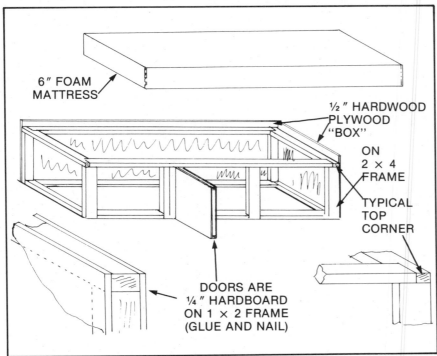

6″ FOAM MATTRESS

½″ HARDWOOD PLYWOOD "BOX"

ON 2 × 4 FRAME

TYPICAL TOP CORNER

DOORS ARE ¼″ HARDBOARD ON 1 × 2 FRAME (GLUE AND NAIL)

Easily-assembled frame of 2 × 4s is covered ¼-inch hardboard that provides smooth surface for application of wallcovering. This design also would lend itself to drawers or cabinets with doors assembled from 1 × 2 stock covered with hardboard.

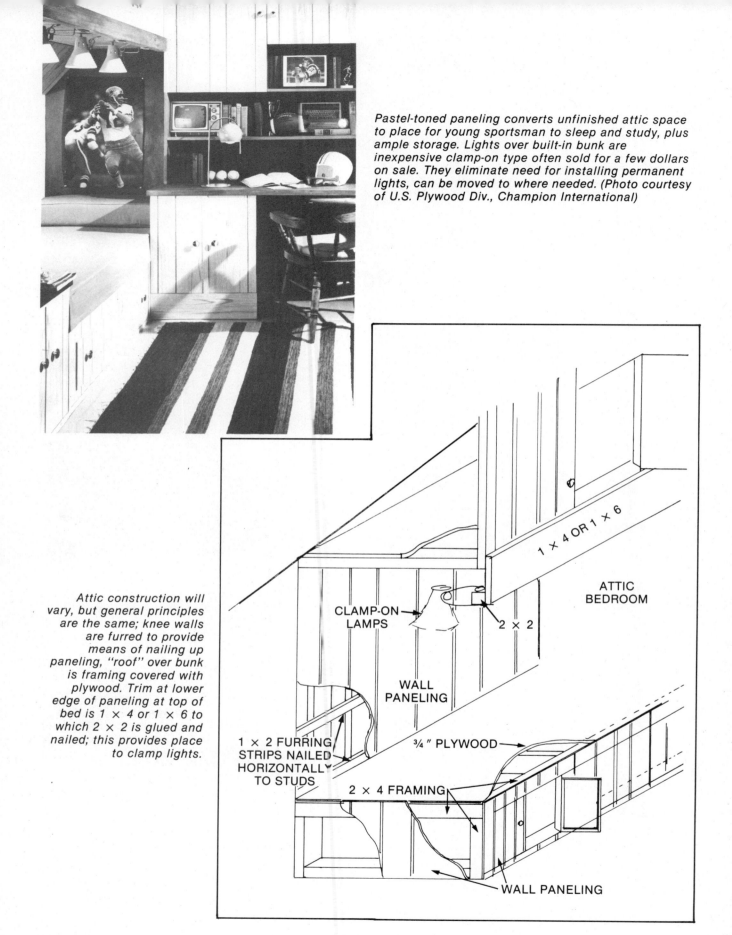

Pastel-toned paneling converts unfinished attic space to place for young sportsman to sleep and study, plus ample storage. Lights over built-in bunk are inexpensive clamp-on type often sold for a few dollars on sale. They eliminate need for installing permanent lights, can be moved to where needed. (Photo courtesy of U.S. Plywood Div., Champion International)

Attic construction will vary, but general principles are the same; knee walls are furred to provide means of nailing up paneling, "roof" over bunk is framing covered with plywood. Trim at lower edge of paneling at top of bed is 1 × 4 or 1 × 6 to which 2 × 2 is glued and nailed; this provides place to clamp lights.

1 × 4 OR 1 × 6

ATTIC BEDROOM

CLAMP-ON LAMPS

2 × 2

WALL PANELING

¾" PLYWOOD

1 × 2 FURRING STRIPS NAILED HORIZONTALLY TO STUDS

2 × 4 FRAMING

WALL PANELING

Less complicated are large boxes mounted on casters that roll on the floor. Strips of wood on the floor can keep the casters aligned with the drawer opening and assure easy action. Build the drawers of 1/2-inch or heavier plywood or particleboard; simply large boxes. The faces of the drawers can be covered with wall paneling or a wallpaper, depending on room decor.

Where a bedroom is really quite small, you might consider utilizing a walk-in closet as a sleep-in alcove. This would be for a youngster, not an adult, of course, as a grown-up would need the closet space. A child can store his or her clothes in a chest of drawers and a tall cabinet for coats and other items that must be stored on hangers.

The room shown has "down-on-the-farm" decor, with rural-patterned wallcovering, a wooden fence for a "headboard" (not quite a "head" board, as it is at the side of the bed). A half-dozen pillows and some stuffed toys convert the bed to a "sofa" during daylight hours. Note that the framing that was originally around the

sliding doors has been left in place, but the inside has been papered to match the rest of the room. You might want to remove the molding, patch any nail holes in the plaster or plasterboard and run the wallcovering right around the corners. The reason this homeowner did not, is that sometime in the future the doors will be returned when the youngster gets older.

For the same reason, you might want to replace the doors to restore the closet if you decided to sell the house. You might also show the house with the bed in the closet and tell prospective buyers you will replace the doors if they would prefer. If they had young children, they might like the idea of the sleeping alcove.

Another way of utilizing every bit of space in a small bedroom is to use ready-made unfinished cabinets and furniture. Select the items to provide the most storage and utility. In the one room shown, a corner desk is flanked by a dressing table with a lift-up top on one side, while cabinets are "stacked" on the other side. The fairly com-

In this girl's bedroom, doors were removed from walk-in closet, regular single bed positioned in it. Trim was left on wall, thus permitting closet to be changed back when room for storage is needed. (Photo courtesy of Wallcovering Information Bureau)

Quick way to create "built-ins" is to buy units of unfinished furniture, fit them around walls of room. Here corner desk is combined with dressing table with lift-up top, storage cabinets with doors and open shelves. (Photo courtesy of Mary Carter Paint Company)

New bedroom in basement provides sleeping and sitting area for two boys. Built-in beds are all but indestructible; mattresses are 5-inch foam units covered with zippered denim slipcovers for easy care. Walls are covered with easy-to-clean hardboard paneling. (Photo courtesy of Masonite Corporation)

pact units provide generous storage space and display shelving, along with a desk for homework and letter writing.

An added touch in this room is a wall covering on the wall at the head of the bed, with a material in a matching pattern used for the spread and a valance on the ceiling positioned a couple of inches from the walls.

If you have converted your basement to living space, including a bedroom for youngsters, the beds also can be built-ins. In the basement bedroom shown, the beds are simple platforms made by cutting 3/4-inch plywood to the required size and trimming the edges of the plywood with 1 × 2s. "Legs" for the outboard ends of the beds

are frames of 1 × 2 covered with paneling. The headboard end of one bed is directly against the wall, while the other bed is a bit longer so the mattress is about a foot away from the wall. The space at the head of the bed is fine for displaying "trophies."

Both beds are used as seating during the day, and the shelf that joins the two beds can serve a multiplicity of functions, including acting as a seat.

A clever touch in the bedroom is a pair of colonial-style doors to close off the basement window. You might want to consider one or two such pairs of doors on other walls as doors to handy cabinets built into interior partitions.

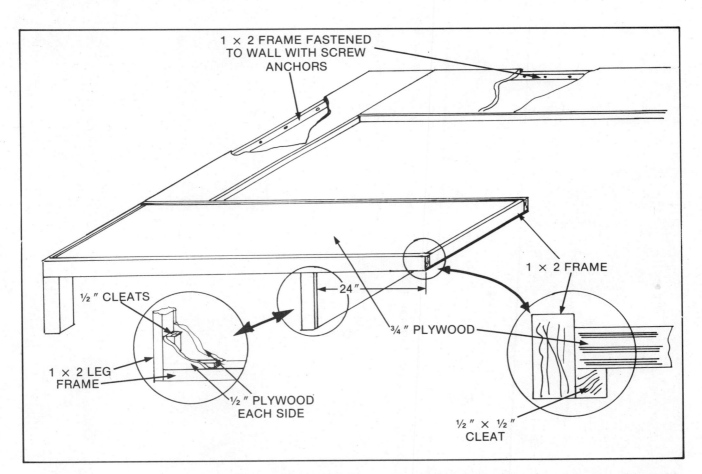

Bunk beds are simply sheets of plywood supported in 1 × 2 frames. One bed is longer than the other, so there is space at the head; shorter bed is nearer doorway to provide walkway into room. Note that "legs" for beds are set back from ends, in "cantilevered" fashion; this could provide storage space also.

Built-ins need not be elaborate. Here shelving is assembled from stock pine shelving stock, glued and nailed with butt joints. Assembly is fitted around window and heat register, and shutters on windows appear to be shelving element. (Photo courtesy of Wallcovering Information Bureau; "Sunshine" pattern wallcovering by Stauffer)

SHELVING

If you don't want to get into projects as ambitious as the ones previously described, you might find a simple shelving arrangement around a window will provide a lot of storage. Buy stock 1 × 6, 1 × 8, 1 × 10 or 1 × 12 pine shelving. If you plan the shelving setup and make a rough drawing, it is quite possible the lumberyard or home center will have a man who can cut the pieces to length for you. Which means you can put it together with hammer and nails, forego any problem with sawdust, and be assured that the boards will have been cut square and true.

All stock shelving lumber is used for this built-in. Have lumberyard cut pieces to sizes you determine before you leave the house. Assemble with white glue and 8-penny finishing nails.

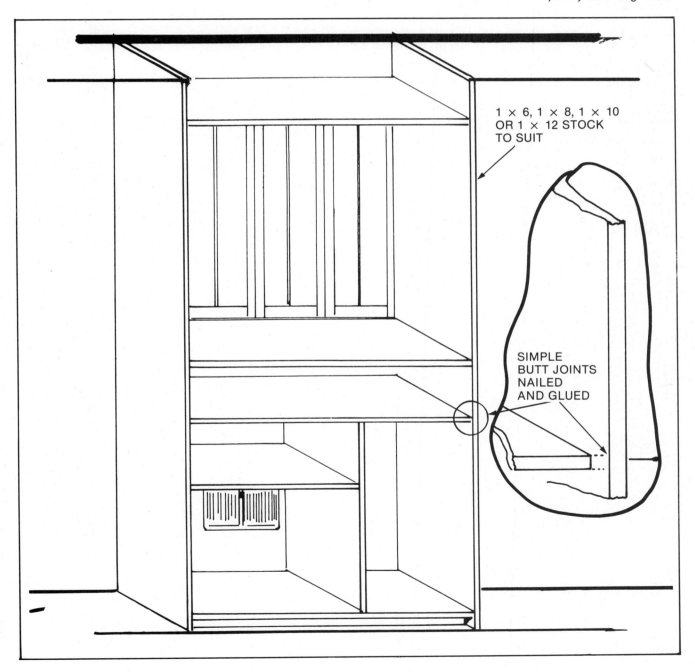

1 × 6, 1 × 8, 1 × 10 OR 1 × 12 STOCK TO SUIT

SIMPLE BUTT JOINTS NAILED AND GLUED

If your assembly stands fairly firmly on the floor, and the floor is level, you will need only a couple of finishing nails or screws driven through the vertical portions of the shelving into the window trim. This makes it easy to remove for painting, papering or moving.

Even a simple shelving layout should have a toe space which is made by nailing a length of 1 × 2 across the back and front of the setup to support the bottom shelf. Set the front 1 × 2 back about 1

inch. If there is a heat register on the wall under the window, as in the room shown, don't forget to allow for it and keep your shelving an inch or two away from it on all sides.

Shutters with movable louvers make the window seem to be a part of the shelving, giving a "cabinet" look when they are closed. The shutters are painted the same color as the shelves.

If desired, you certainly could stain and varnish the shelves and shutters.

6 The Home Office

CABINETS

Some of us don't have a separate room for an office, and even a desk would take up too much space. In this situation, a two-cabinet office might be the answer. These cabinets look like ordinary pieces of furniture—just a couple of chests of drawers than can be styled to fit in any room in the house. In a bedroom, they can be used as night stands, in a living room they will appear to be a couple of end tables.

One of the cabinets is basically a two-drawer file unit, sized to hold regular letter-size file holders. The companion piece has a typewriter under a lid, with the typewriter at the proper height for comfortable typing. The false drawer fronts below the typewriter compartment hide space for the storage of office supplies. The design of the cabinet offers necessary knee space for typing, and a slide-out shelf and a fold-up shelf can add work space.

When cabinets are closed, the office "disappears" and units appear to be two small cabinets with different-size drawers. (Photo courtesy of Phil McCafferty)

Note that the hinged top conceals a portable typewriter in operating position. If the typewriter is a long-carriage portable, it will have to be positioned sideways to permit closing the top. If you want a standard typewriter to fit, the cabinet will have to be made larger. In that case, the other cabinet also should be enlarged so it would match in size.

You can build the cabinets of glued-up solid stock, if you want to match other furniture in a room, or use a hardwood-plywood. The units shown are assembled from ¾-inch hardwood plywood.

Sliding Shelf

Be sure to check the fit and try the sliding shelf in the typing cabinet before installing the wooden cleats that create the slides. There must be some clearance between the slides to permit easy movement, but too much will let the slide angle down when it is pulled out the full length. Add a

Two-cabinet office consists basically of two plywood boxes. One has lift-up lid with four sides that conceals typewriter, plus several shelves. Other cabinet has two full-size file drawers to complete office.

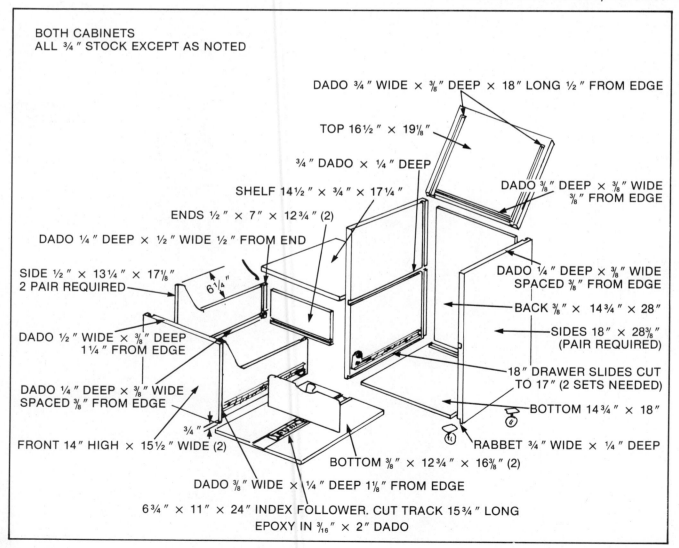

BOTH CABINETS
ALL ¾″ STOCK EXCEPT AS NOTED

DADO ¾″ WIDE × ⅜″ DEEP × 18″ LONG ½″ FROM EDGE

TOP 16½″ × 19⅛″

¾″ DADO × ¼″ DEEP

SHELF 14½″ × ¾″ × 17¼″

ENDS ½″ × 7″ × 12¾″ (2)

DADO ¼″ DEEP × ½″ WIDE ½″ FROM END

DADO ⅜″ DEEP × ⅜″ WIDE ⅜″ FROM EDGE

SIDE ½″ × 13¼″ × 17⅛″ 2 PAIR REQUIRED

6¼″

DADO ¼″ DEEP × ⅜″ WIDE SPACED ⅜″ FROM EDGE

BACK ⅜″ × 14¾″ × 28″

DADO ½″ WIDE × ⅜″ DEEP 1¼″ FROM EDGE

SIDES 18″ × 28⅜″ (PAIR REQUIRED)

DADO ¼″ DEEP × ⅜″ WIDE SPACED ⅜″ FROM EDGE

18″ DRAWER SLIDES CUT TO 17″ (2 SETS NEEDED)

¾″

BOTTOM 14¾″ × 18″

FRONT 14″ HIGH × 15½″ WIDE (2)

RABBET ¾″ WIDE × ¼″ DEEP

BOTTOM ⅜″ × 12¾″ × 16⅜″ (2)

DADO ⅜″ WIDE × ¼″ DEEP 1⅛″ FROM EDGE

6¾″ × 11″ × 24″ INDEX FOLLOWER. CUT TRACK 15¾″ LONG
EPOXY IN 3/16″ × 2″ DADO

stop block to prevent the shelf from being pulled all the way out; it can be screwed to the underside of the shelf after it has been slipped into the opening in the side of the cabinet.

Drop-down Shelf

The drop-down shelf is held by a length of piano (continuous) hinge for maximum support, and the door of the cabinet also is pivoted on a piano hinge. These hinges can be purchased in various lengths, then cut to the correct length with a hacksaw. Further support for the hinged shelf is provided by a locking support that pivots down when the shelf is lowered. Be sure the support does not interfere with anything that is fitted into the paper pocket attached to the lower part of the inside of the door. Which means you want the support as short as possible, but long enough to provide adequate support. The paper pocket is made by cutting grooves into two lengths of 1 × 2 to accept a scrap of hardboard or paneling ⅛ or ¼

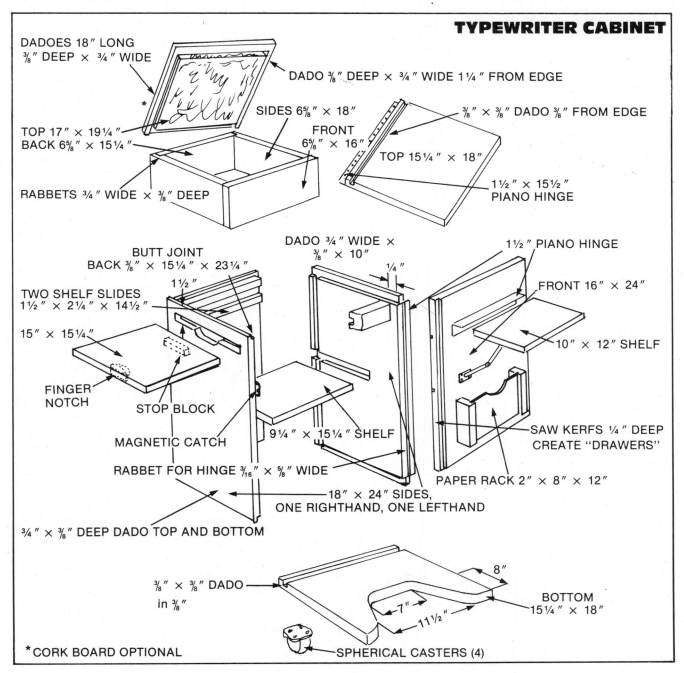

TYPEWRITER CABINET

DADOES 18″ LONG ⅜″ DEEP × ¾″ WIDE

DADO ⅜″ DEEP × ¾″ WIDE 1¼″ FROM EDGE

SIDES 6⅝″ × 18″

FRONT 6⅝″ × 16″

⅜″ × ⅜″ DADO ⅜″ FROM EDGE

TOP 15¼″ × 18″

TOP 17″ × 19¼″
BACK 6⅝″ × 15¼″

1½″ × 15½″ PIANO HINGE

RABBETS ¾″ WIDE × ⅜″ DEEP

BUTT JOINT
BACK ⅜″ × 15¼″ × 23¼″

DADO ¾″ WIDE × ⅜″ × 10″

1½″

¼″

1½″ PIANO HINGE

TWO SHELF SLIDES 1½″ × 2¼″ × 14½″

FRONT 16″ × 24″

15″ × 15¼″

10″ × 12″ SHELF

FINGER NOTCH

STOP BLOCK

MAGNETIC CATCH

9¼″ × 15¼″ SHELF

SAW KERFS ¼″ DEEP CREATE "DRAWERS"

RABBET FOR HINGE ³⁄₁₆″ × ⅝″ WIDE

PAPER RACK 2″ × 8″ × 12″

18″ × 24″ SIDES, ONE RIGHTHAND, ONE LEFTHAND

¾″ × ⅜″ DEEP DADO TOP AND BOTTOM

⅜″ × ⅜″ DADO in ⅜″

8″

BOTTOM 15¼″ × 18″

7″

11½″

*CORK BOARD OPTIONAL

SPHERICAL CASTERS (4)

L-shape top over this cabinet is covered with plastic laminate for long wear, easy cleaning. Most of the time the counter and cabinet are for the children; occasionally Mom or Dad can use the unit for a desk or hobby surface. (Photo courtesy of Azrock Floor Products)

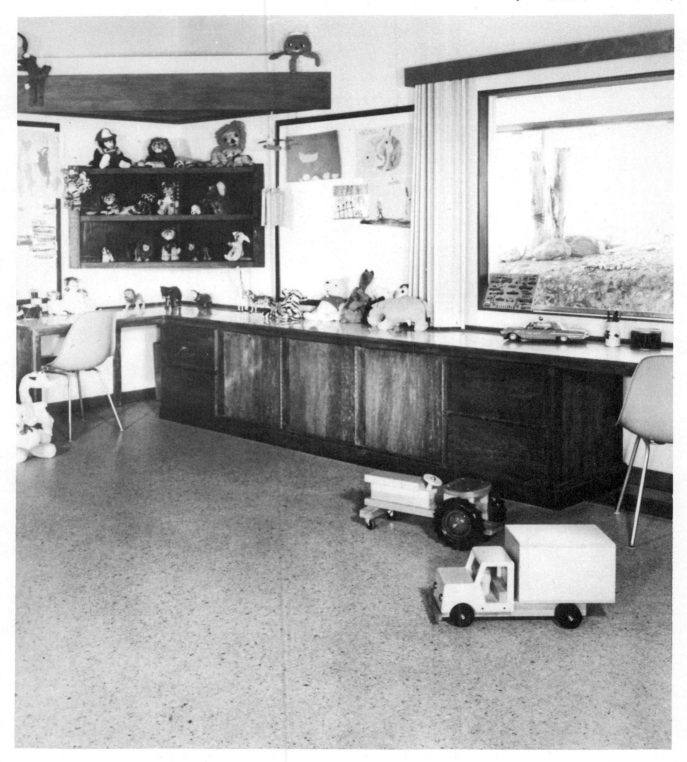

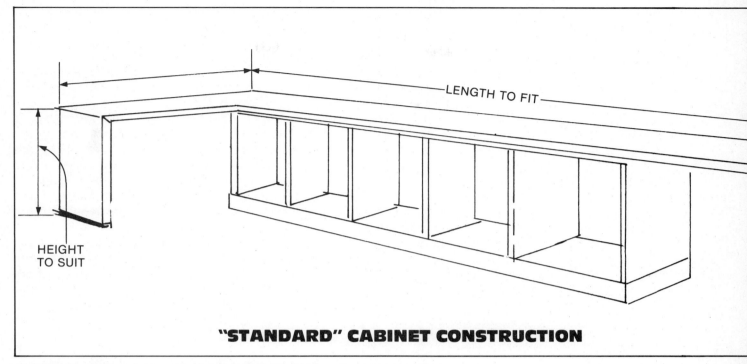

"STANDARD" CABINET CONSTRUCTION

Child/adult cabinet and counter top is made like kitchen base cabinet. Drawers are "standard" construction supported on ball-bearing slides, doors can be hinged on piano hinges or may be sliding type to save room.

inch thick. The bottom of the pocket is another scrap that is glued and nailed to the lower ends of the 1 × 2s.

Construction

For the back of the cabinet use a piece of ⅜-inch plywood fitted into dadoes cut ⅜ inch in from the back edge. A rabbet in the upper edge of each side of the cabinet holds the top on which the typewriter sets. Support the front of the top on a brace fitted between the sides, and put a duplicate brace across the back. Cut a dado the length of each brace to create the slides. These braces (cleats) must be fitted to the sliding shelf before they are installed.

Notch the bottom of the typing cabinet to provide foot and knee room when you type, yet still leave some shelf for storage.

To create the look of drawers, the door of the cabinet is kerfed ¼ inch deep. The "drawers" can be spaced to suit, the the larger one should be at the bottom to look best.

The cabinet for the file drawers is a basic plywood box cabinet, very similar to the kitchen cabinet. Install ball-bearing drawer slides to provide easy movement of the drawers. The horizontal partition between the drawers does not support the top drawer—the ball-bearing slides do that—it simply reinforces the basic cabinet. A brace across the top between the sides adds further strength. Note that the sides of the top drawer must clear this brace, so be sure the sides are a little more than ¾ inch below the top of the drawer front. The same kind of clearance is required for the bottom drawer to miss the middle shelf.

Hardware

While not absolutely necessary, slide followers for the file drawers certainly help keep the folders upright and easy to pick out when needed. You buy these metal devices from mail-order outlets such as Albert Constantine and Craftsman Wood Service. Cut the slide portion with a hacksaw to fit inside the drawers, then secure it to the dado in the drawer bottom.

Drawer pulls should be selected to be compatible with the hardware in the room in which the cabinets are located. Spherical casters are best for the cabinets, as they roll easily, even on carpeting. And it might be necessary to roll the cabinets to another room on occasion, over carpeting.

WORK SURFACES

Here we offer a surface that can be used by both adults and youngsters: an L-shape top fitted over a long cabinet on one wall, supported by an end panel. The top is covered with plastic laminate (or ceramic tile) for a long-wearing surface. There is space for knees and a chair under the extended top that goes around the corner, and this space might even double for occasional record-keeping for a home office.

The cabinet shown also has an extension of the top on the long cabinet, so there are two places for a chair. If you have room only on one wall for a long cabinet, then do allow an open space with an opening under the top.

You might want more than the four drawers shown; this plan has two at each end of the cabinet. Keep in mind, however, that these are big, deep drawers, and there is a tendency to overload them. Overloading makes it tough to pull them out and to shove them back. Three smaller drawers might be a better idea than the two larger ones.

Doors on the cabinets shown are hung on piano (continuous) hinges, which will stand up to the rough handling of youngsters. Alternately, where space is a problem, consider sliding doors that take up no room space. You might even prefer

Simple Solutions... Create a Desk in an afternoon

them over hinged doors as long as you realize that some youngsters tend to forget to close doors, and another child making a quick move can run into one of them.

If you do stay with just two drawers, by all means use ball-bearing slides. These slides can be obtained to handle 50, 100, 150 pounds and more, so choose the unit that will handle the expected load. It also is easy to lift out drawers fitted with the slides. This comes in handy when it is necessary to repair them, or if you want to carry the contents to another part of the room.

DESKS

One quick project is a "sawhorse" picnic table that can be converted into a desk or work table. If the table is a bit high, cut all four legs by the same amount to lower it. If the top is rough lumber,

cover it with a sheet of tempered hardboard. For an ordinary desk, simply glue the hardboard to the top, using a few brads to hold it until the glue sets.

When the table is to be used for a hobby—such as model-making—where the surface eventually will become scratched, cut and scarred, glue a sheet of newspaper between the top and the hardboard. Spread white glue on the table, place the newspaper on it, then apply a coat of glue to it and put the hardboard over the glue. Clamp the hardboard or place weights on it until the glue sets, which should be about 24 hours. Use $\frac{1}{8}$ or $\frac{1}{4}$-inch tempered hardboard with one smooth side. In the future, to replace the marred surface slip a putty knife between the table top and hardboard and lift it up . . . it will come off quite easily.

The side that has been glued will be difficult to clean, so don't try to use a hardboard with two good sides on the assumption that the side that is

Opposite: A home office contained in a closet! The work top is supported by two file cabinets and is well lighted by fluorescent tubes that are plant lights that simulate sunshine. Here is a perfect solution for lack of work space, and one which can disappear when company comes. The pegboard above supplies usable shelf space for desk accessories and books.

This do-it-yourself built-in includes full length shelves supported by inexpensive brackets, the desk has a Formica counter which is supported by files. (Window Shade Manufacturers Association)

"Sawhorse" picnic table is easily converted for use as desk in informal (casual) decor by applying sheet of hardboard to the top to create surface for writing or hobby work. (Photo courtesy Wallcovering Industry Bureau—General Tire Wallcovering)

Author's office has L-shape desk made by joining two hollow-core doors at right angle. Ends are supported on metal file cabinets that are antiqued, as is top. Wooden cleats screwed to wall, plus ready-made leg, support the desk at the corner.

down can later be turned up and used. Hardboard with two good sides can be used if the surface will see service only as a writing surface, or for any hobby that will not scar the surface. After a few years the hardboard can then be lifted and turned over to provide a fresh, clean surface.

Another quick and easy means of creating a home office is the "old door trick." that is, you purchase a couple of hollow-core interior doors from your local lumberyard or home center for a few dollars apiece. These will be "rejects" that cannot be sold to be used as doors because there are stains in the wood, or the edges are chipped or there is some other very visible flaw that makes them unsuitable for a home. These flaws in no way interfere with their suitability as desks.

L-Shape Desk

I have in my home office a large L-shape desk made of two doors set atop several file cabinets. To support the corner where the two doors join, a block is screwed to each adjacent wall. The blocks, assembled from two pieces of 1 × 2 stock, enable you to drive screws up into the doors to hold them in position. The "outside" corner of the two doors is supported by a ready-made leg.

To support the two doors absolutely level, it was necessary to trim the leg a bit to make it fit snugly under the corner. A wood screw was driven down through the doors in countersunk holes, into the top of the leg. A little wood putty was applied and sanded flush. To make the desk appear to be all one unit, the doors were "antiqued", as were the file cabinets.

A small, three-door chest was built of 1 × 2's and covered with leftover wall paneling, so the chest would match the walls. As described in the chapter on using plywood, utilizing a frame of solid stock permits use of a thin material as a covering for the chest. This type of shelf is handy for office supplies, such as boxes of paper that would crowd a file cabinet. The shelf above the desk is a frame of 1 × 2 lumber with paneling on the top, bottom and edges. Two metal shelf brackets are screwed to the wall to provide support for the shelf. One advantage of the shelf, since it just sits on the brackets, is that when it gets overloaded and bows down it can be reversed with the bow up so it gradually becomes level again.

"Built-ins" in this room are recesses in the wall, and a simple shelf across one end that doubles as a serving buffet for parties. Recesses were created by making a wall of 2 × 12s (space was available), then framing in openings and covering the inside with plasterboard that was given a coat of textured paint, the same shown on the walls. Platform for fireplace is plywood box covered with fireproof simulated bricks. (Photo courtesy of The Fireplace Institute)

For instructions on how you can set up this shelving system, see the diagram in Chapter 2. (Photo courtesy of Hedrich-Blessing)

Cabinet framing is stained a light color to match paneling on walls, while doors and drawer fronts are made from darker-stained hardwood-plywood for contrast. (Photo courtesy of Armstrong Cork Co.).

Book shelves on the wall of this room are a simple assembly of pine shelving stock. Metal brackets are screwed to vertical partitions to hold metal clips that support shelves at desired spacing. The lamp table is a plywood box to which Z-Brick is adhered. A glass top completes this table, which can be readily dis-assembled for moving. (Photo courtesy of Z-Brick Co.)

Built-ins can mean the
difference between spacious
comfort and cluttered
disorganization. Sliding doors
reveal hidden shelves in
shallow and deep closets.

Stock used to make standard bookcases is also used to build storage cabinet with
decorative ready-made patterns. Top of cabinet serves as display counter. (Photo
courtesy of Hedrich-Blessing)

Colored pegboard adds a bright note and offers flexibility for storing odd-sized items. (Photo courtesy of Masonite Corp.)

With the two cabinets open and ready for work, you have a handy typewriter desk, slide-out and lift-up shelves for additional storage, and a small shelf for even more. The other cabinet shown has generous file drawers for standard letter-size file folders. (Photo courtesy of Phil McCafferty)

7 How to Work with Plywood

Probably no building material is as versatile as plywood, and for the home craftsman the large, flat panels provide an inexpensive, extremely strong wood product that can be used in hundreds of projects.

The cross-laminated veneer construction of plywood provides much more stability than lumber, which is subject to twisting, cupping, and warping. Plywood may be used for paneling, partitions, doors, furniture, cabinets and built-ins, shelving, fences and wind screens, patio decking, outdoor storage units and projects beyond count.

CHARACTERISTICS

For the home craftsman there are two basic types of plywood: interior grade and exterior grade. The interior type has a water-resistant glue used between the laminations, while exterior-grade plywood has glue that is completely waterproof.

For cabinets and built-ins the interior grade is fine, with the exception that an exterior-grade plywood should be used on countertops that will be subjected to a lot of moisture. Plastic laminate or ceramic tile generally will prevent moisture from reaching the plywood on which it is applied, but if you find that any counter on which you work shows signs of water damage to the top, use exterior-grade plywood when you replace the top.

Birch plywood used for cabinets, or any hardwood-faced plywood, will come with one "good" side and one "bad" side. In the case of hardwood-plywood, however, both sides are free of knots, splits and checks, and either side can be exposed.

Grades

Softwood plywood comes in grades, such as A—A, A—B and so on. For most construction, where one side will not be seen, A—D is all right. Where the inside of a cabinet will be seen occasionally, an A—C or A—B should be used. The various letters means this: A-grade is smooth and paintable, with neatly-made repairs permissable. Grade B is solid-surface veneer with circular repair plugs and some knots permitted. When you get to C-grade, there can be knotholes to 1 inch and occasional knotholes 1½ inches, providing the total width of all knots and knotholes within a specified section do not exceed certain limits. Limited splits are permitted. C-grade plgd (plugged) is an improved C-grade with splits limited to ⅛ inch in width and knotholes and borer holes limited to ¼ × ½ inch. The poorest grade is D-grade, for which knots and knotholes up to 2½ inches in width and even larger are permitted within certain limits. Limited splits are permitted.

The grade marks on plywood will help you choose the kind you want, but a glance at both sides of a sheet will quickly tell you if it will be suitable for the job you have in mind.

WORKING WITH PLYWOOD

As with any kind of work, planning is important when you use plywood. If you will make a lot of cuts in a sheet, first make a rough working drawing so you can get an idea of how you can cut with the least waste. Keep in mind that most projects will require that the good face grain runs the long way of any piece you cut. And don't forget to allow for the saw kerf, which usually is about ⅛ inch. If you overlook that ⅛ inch and cut four pieces, you already are ½ inch off.

Plywood is still the "basic" wood product used by both professional and home craftsmen. Its great strength makes it ideal as roof decking, wall sheathing, subflooring, and for cabinets and built-ins.

All photos in this chapter are courtesy of American Plywood Association.

When sawing plywood, the idea is to have the good face positioned so the teeth of the blade cut into it. With a handsaw this means the good face up, and the same is true when cutting on a table saw. With a radial-arm saw the good face is up when you crosscut, as the blade is pulled back through the stock in a "climbing" cut. When you rip on a radial-arm saw, the good face is down, as the blade then cuts on the "upstroke."

A portable electric saw also cuts upward, so the good face of the plywood should be positioned down. An electric jig saw (saber saw) cuts on the upstroke also, so the good face should be down, and all marking done on the back side of the plywood.

If you must plane the edges of plywood, make sure the plane blade is very sharp, and take shallow cuts. Plane from each end of an edge toward the middle to avoid splintering at the ends. The use of a planer or plywood blade will produce a cut that is so smooth it won't even need sanding. If at all possible it is best to avoid planing. It sometimes is necessary, however, to plane the edges of plywood doors when fitting them.

When cutting plywood with a handsaw, have the "good" side up, and support the panel so it doesn't sag. The saw should have 10 to 15 points per inch. If you want to minimize splintering on the back side, clamp a piece of scrap lumber to the plywood and cut it along with the plywood.

When cross-cutting or ripping on a table saw, or cross-cutting on a radial-arm saw, the "good" side of plywood should be up. When ripping on a radial-arm saw, the good side is down. The basic idea is to have the good side facing into the teeth of the blade as it rotates.

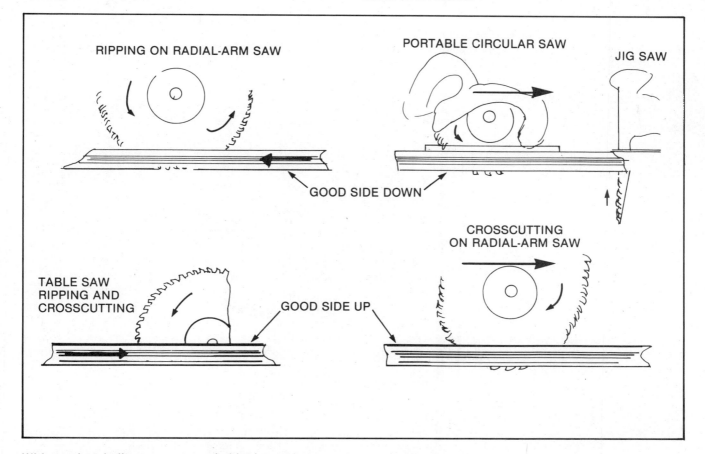

RIPPING ON RADIAL-ARM SAW

PORTABLE CIRCULAR SAW

JIG SAW

GOOD SIDE DOWN

TABLE SAW RIPPING AND CROSSCUTTING

GOOD SIDE UP

CROSSCUTTING ON RADIAL-ARM SAW

With an electric jig saw, put good side down; the same is true when using a portable circular saw.

If it is necessary to plane the edges of plywood, as when fitting a cabinet door, use a sharp plane and work from each end toward the middle; this will avoid splintering. In most cases, if a sharp plywood or planer blade is used, planing will not be necessary because the cut will be smooth.

Butt joints are simplest to make, as at left, and often are used with ¾-inch plywood. When thinner material is used you should include a glue block inside the corner, as at right.

Joints

Even the very best glue cannot make up for a sloppy joint, so "dry-fit" pieces of a project together to make sure they meet properly. When using ¾-inch plywood, or thicker, you can glue and then nail or screw plain butt joints. If the plywood is thinner, then use a glue block inside each corner. The use of framing made from solid stock permits using lighter plywood, which enables you to keep down the weight. Thinner plywood also is less expensive, so you can save money—as long as you don't spend too much on the framing stock.

Rabbet joints provide a bit of extra gluing surface and are quite neat, as only a thin edge of the plywood shows. The miter joint (not shown here) is the neatest, but does require precision cutting at the correct angle, and proper fastening.

If you have a table or radial-arm saw, dadoes make neat joints for slide-in shelves in cabinets. Use a dado blade to make the cut in one pass, both for width and depth. With some care, and a fence clamped to the plywood, you can use a portable circular saw to cut the grooves, using a dado blade.

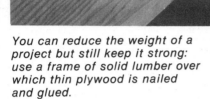

You can reduce the weight of a project but still keep it strong: use a frame of solid lumber over which thin plywood is nailed and glued.

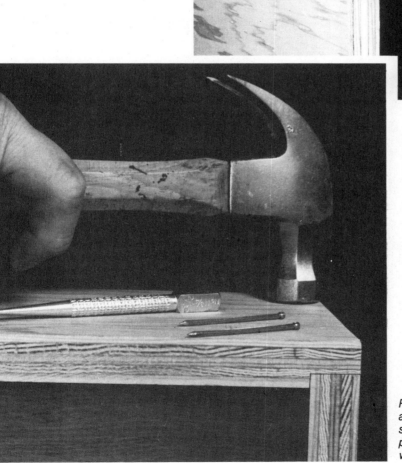

Dado joints made with a power saw enable production of neat shelves. Dado blade, either the multi-blade type or the newer adjustable types, make the dadoes in one pass. Make the dadoes a "sliding" fit; it should not be necessary to hammer the shelves into the slots.

Rabbet joints are neat and strong, and provide additional gluing surfaces. Any permanent joint in plywood should be glued; ordinary white glue is fine for most jobs.

101

Nail size is determined by the thickness of the plywood. For ¾-inch plywood, use 6-penny casing nails or 8-penny finishing nails. With ⅝-inch plywood, drive 6 or 8-penny finishing or casing nails. When ½-inch plywood is being nailed, use 4-penny or 6-penny nails. When nailing ⅜-inch material, nail sizes are 3 or 4 penny. You can drive ¾ or 1-inch brads or 3-penny finishing nails to attach ¼-inch plywood. Where the material will not show, you may use 1-inch blue lath nails.

Nailing Plywood Joints

On some projects where nails will be near the edges, predrilling is a good idea. Use a drill bit slightly smaller than the nail diameter, or use a nail with the head cut off as the "bit". Hand or electric drill can be used.

For most projects, space the nails about 6 inches apart. When you are using thinner plywood, say over framing, space the nails closer to avoid any buckling, and always use glue.

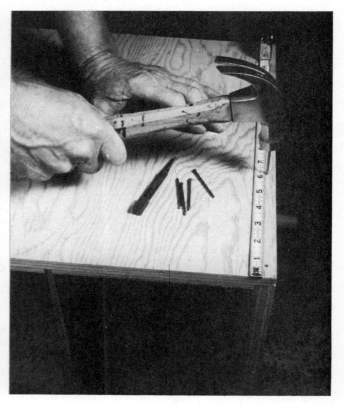

Glue and Fasteners

All plywood joints should include glue as well as fasteners, unless the project is one that will occasionally, or frequently, be disassembled. Nail size is determined by the thickness of the plywood. Finishing nails are used usually, but casing nails that are like oversize finishing nails are used for extra strength. When nailing close to an edge, predrill the nail holes with a bit that is slightly smaller than the nail diameter. Drill just through the first piece of plywood and start into the second. Nails are spaced 6 inches apart for most projects, but closer spacing is required for thinner plywood to prevent slight buckling between nails. Once again, be sure to use glue as well as nails.

For a really strong joint, use flathead wood screws. Both screws and nails should be countersunk and the heads covered with wood putty. Or, use plugs cut from scraps of plywood. Pieces of dowel will make a contrast to the plywood and create a pegged "colonial" look to the project.

One quick and easy way to hold miter joints is to use plain corrugated fasteners at each end. Sheet metal screws are better for some joints than wood screws (as with particleboard) although you cannot get them as long as wood

Flathead wood screws are used when you want a joint that is stronger than one made with nails. A No. 8 screw is used on ⅝ and ¾-inch plywood, No. 6 with ⅜ and ½-inch plywood and No. 4 screws are used with ¼-inch plywood. Use the longest screw practical; this will depend, of course, on the thickness of the backing material.

All nails and screws should be countersunk and heads covered with wood putty. Fill the holes so the putty is above the surface, then sand it flush when it dries. If screws drive hard, wipe them on a bar of soap or a piece of paraffin.

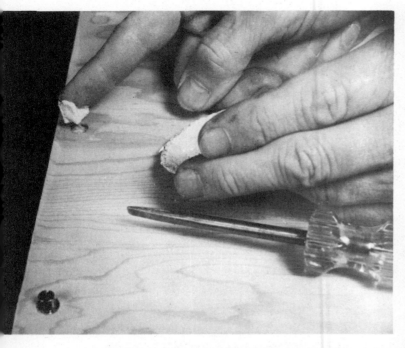

Ordinary corrugated fasteners can be driven into a corner to hold a miter while the glue sets, and it also provides reinforcement for the joint. Use one at each end where possible.

"Dry-assemble" a project to check for proper fit of all joints, then disassemble and apply glue. White glue is sufficient for most projects, but if using waterproof exterior-grade plywood, apply a two-part waterproof glue.

screws, and greater length is required for some joints. Where really great strength is required, use nuts and bolts. This also is true of items that need to be disassembled for moving.

For most jobs, ordinary white glue is fine. "Carpenter's" glue is a bit stronger and has a quicker "tack," when that is required. For outdoor assemblies made with exterior-grade plywood, definitely use a two-part waterproof glue that is mixed just before it is used. Both white glue and carpenter's glue are water-resistant, but not waterproof, and will fail when exposed to constant weathering, rain and snow.

Edge grain of plywood soaks up glue quickly, so apply one coat and let it get tacky, then apply a second coat just before you joint the pieces. Screws or nails will hold a joint once they are driven, but during assembly regular clamps will assure that you get the project square and the joints tight. Nails or screws then will hold the joints tightly after the glue has set and the clamps have been removed.

When you hang cabinets on a stud wall, use a thin plywood back in the cabinet, and screws can be driven through the back into the wall studs through the plaster or plasterboard. For hollow

Apply glue with a brush or stick, or directly from the container in the case of white glue. End grain absorbs glue quickly, so apply a light coat, let it dry for a few minutes and then apply a second coat just before assembling the joints.

While nails and screws will draw a glued joint together, clamps make an even tighter connection. Use shims of cardboard or wood under the clamp pads to prevent marring the plywood.

Standard stud walls allow hanging cabinets by driving screws through the cabinet backs into the studs. Locate one stud by tapping on the wall, then measure 16 inches to find the next. The 16-inch spacing is not always consistent near a corner or next to a door or window.

masonry walls, use toggle bolts or "Molly" anchors. The "Molly" devices permit removing and replacing the screw, while the toggle portion of a toggle bolt drops inside the wall when the screw is removed.

For poured concrete and other solid masonry, you can use "glue-on" holders that have nails or screws that project for attachment. Also, there now are cartridge-actuated nail and stud drivers that can be rented to attach furring strips to masonry. The cabinet or other item is then attached to the furring strips with wood screws.

If you are hanging cabinets on hollow masonry walls, you will need to use toggle bolts or "Molly" fasteners as shown. The advantage of the "Molly" fastener is that you can remove and replace the screw once the fastener is in place.

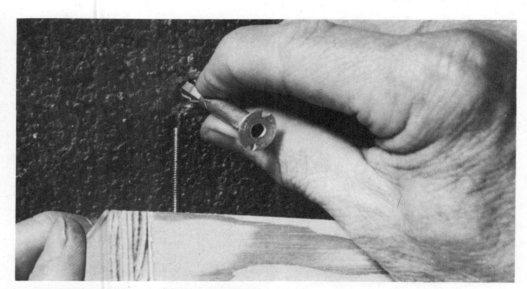

On poured concrete and other solid masonry, "glue-on" masonry anchors are required. Some types are simply projecting nails onto which the wood is driven, then the nail clinched over. The fastener shown is a threaded screw, and the nut is turned on it to hold cabinet to wall.

Hinges

Door hardware for plywood should be a type that permits driving the screws into face grain; screws driven into edge grain do not have much strength. "H-hinges" and "H-L" hinges are strong and provide a "colonial" or "early-American" look to a project. As shown, for larger doors where three hinges are required, use a pair of "H-L" hinges, with an "H-hinge" at the center.

Semi-concealed hinges do a nice job on lipped

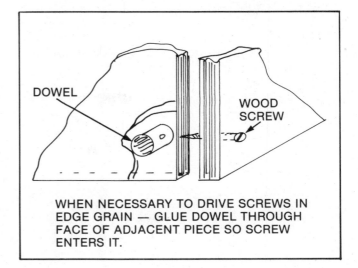

WHEN NECESSARY TO DRIVE SCREWS IN EDGE GRAIN — GLUE DOWEL THROUGH FACE OF ADJACENT PIECE SO SCREW ENTERS IT.

Surface-mounted hinges are attached easily and require no mortising and add a decorative touch. One pair of H or H-L hinges are sufficient for most cabinet doors. For larger doors, use a pair of H-L hinges with H-hinge in middle.

cabinet doors, and the screws are driven into the face grain for good strength. Semi-concealed loose-pin hinges (which permit easy removal of the door by pulling the pins) show only the pin barrel when the door is closed, and thus look like regular butt hinges. Screws, however, again are driven into face grain for good holding strength. Hinges with concealed pins mount on the sides of a cabinet, so that no facing frame is necessary. They are ideal for a cabinet of "modern" design. Only the pivot is visible from the front when the door is closed.

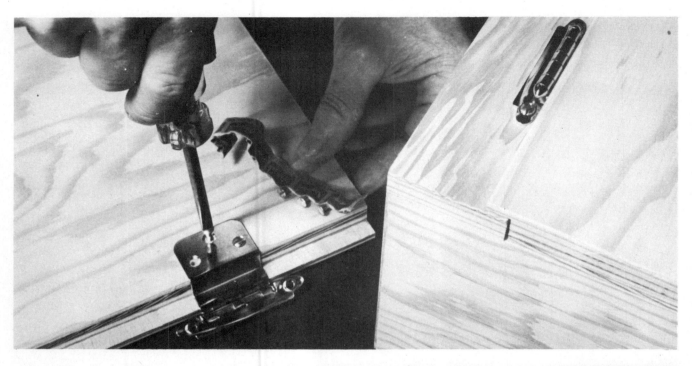

Lipped, overlapping doors hang neatly with semi-concealed hinges. These offset hinges are ideal for plywood, as the screws all are driven into face grain. The edge grain of plywood does not provide the holding strength of face grain.

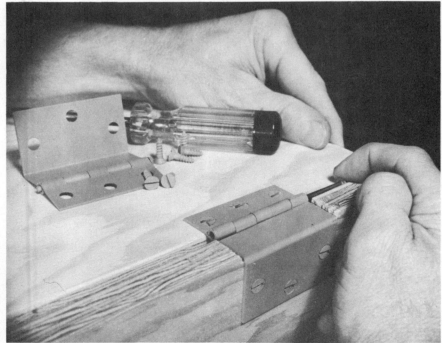

Loose-pin hinges that are semi-concealed look much like ordinary butt hinges when the door is closed, because only the barrel shows. Again, the screws are driven into the face grain of the plywood to provide excellent holding power.

When mounted directly onto the cabinet side, concealed-pin hinges provide a neat modern appearance to flush doors. Because no facing frame is required with this type of hinge, cabinet construction is simplified. Only the pivot is visible from the front with the door closed. A pair of these hinges is used for a small door, and three for a larger door. Three hinges are called a "pair and a half".

Painted kitchen cabinets often are made from dense particleboard. The type used for cabinetmaking has close-packed small flakes near surface, so it can be sealed and painted easily. (Photo courtesy of Armstrong Cork Company)

8
How to
Work with
Particleboard

Because the average home craftsman doesn't know much about it, particleboard is not much used for home projects such as cabinets, although the manufacturers of furniture and other products have considered it their favorite material for quality items for quite a few years.

First, what is particleboard? This man-made material is created by mixing particles of wood with a resin binder, then compressing the mixture and heating it to produce a uniformly dense panel. The light tan panels are flat, have no grain, and are completely free of knots.

Edges of particleboard are tight, with no voids as occur in softwood plywood. Particleboard is heavy for a wood product; you'll notice the first time you pick up a panel. It's about 40 percent heavier per volume than pine lumber, and 25 percent more than softwood plywood. Both sides of particleboard are smooth.

There are some disadvantages to particleboard, as no material can be all things to every craftsman. Comparing particleboard to some other cabinetmaking materials in 3/4-inch panels of 4 × 8 feet, we find that particleboard has a higher surface hardness than A—B softwood plywood, A—2 birch plywood, and 1-inch (3/4 inch net) pine lumber of clear and better grade. When it comes to workability, soft pine lumber is easier than particleboard to saw, plane, rout and drill. Because of the glue lines, both kinds of plywood are more difficult than particleboard to work. However, although particleboard can be worked with regular tools, the resin in it makes it tougher on cutting edges.

Stability of particleboard is very good. It orginally was developed for manufacturers of table tops, cabinet doors and cabinet tops who demanded an inexpensive, stable wood core for their products.

Vertical compression strength, is also good. To compare horizontal strength with that of other materials, consider this comparison: pine shelving will support a load on 36 inch centers; plywood is safe on 30 inch centers; particleboard is heavier and has shorter wood fibers and so requires spacing of no more than 24 inches for the same load. On 24 inch centers a ¾ inch particleboard will support 70 pounds per square foot and deflect just ¼ inch. This kind of strength is more than adequate for a set of heavy encyclopedias.

When it comes to comparison of edge finishing, lumber has a clear superiority. Edges are smooth and tight and require no filling, although end grain may in some cases. Particleboard, however, comes in second. You can sometimes obtain it with filled round or square edges, or with applied wood edges. Plywood would be last choice, for it has voids that need to be filled, and there is edge grain that must be concealed by filling, with veneer tape or solid wood.

Another advantage: particleboard normally can be stained or painted with no additional preparation. For a top-notch job, wipe the surface with thinned paste filler and sand it. Plywood and lumber have problems of raised grain, and you have to work to hide color differences in solid lumber. Patches and repairs on softwood plywood are difficult to conceal except by painting.

Cost

When it comes to dollars and cents, the cost of particleboard can make you a confirmed user in a hurry. According to Louisiana-Pacific, a major producer of lumber, plywood and particleboard, the price of plywood with two good sides is more than double the same size piece of particleboard. When you compare it with the same amount of pine lumber, you are talking three times the cost.

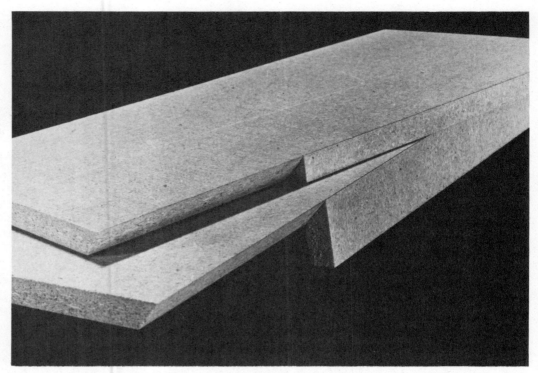

With a sharp blade on a table or radial-arm saw, a "self-edge" is relatively easy to develop. Note that the bottom self-edge would be ideal to increase front thickness of a countertop.

Molding can be used to edge particleboard. From top to bottom: outside-corner trim; plain screen trim; half-round molding; ¾-inch cove molding for ¾-inch particleboard. Use of moldings eliminates need for filling and finishing rough particle-board edges.

Photos courtesy Louisiana - Pacific

Birch plywood is about four times the price of particleboard.

Selection

Particleboard is made in thicknesses from 1/8 to 2 inches. Panels can be as wide as 5 feet and as long as 26 feet. Density of the product can range from 28 to 62 pounds per cubic foot. During the manufacturing and blending of the panel materials, wood preservatives, termite-resistant chemicals and even substances to make the particleboard fire-resistant may be added.

Furniture manufacturers use particleboard in both high- and low-priced items for core stock to be painted or varnished. It also is used under plastic laminate, sheet vinyl and wood veneer. Because it is uniformly dense, it makes an ideal material for cabinets for hi-fi speakers.

Most specialty boards are not sold in your local lumberyard. What you can find are medium-density boards from 42 to 45 pounds per cubic foot in 4 × 8-foot panels of standard thicknesses. These thicknesses are 3/8, 1/2, 5/8 and 3/4 inch, with 5/8 inch being the most commonly available.

WORKING WITH PARTICLEBOARD

When you work with particleboard two things quickly become obvious, especially if working with power tools: first, instead of sawdust that presents little problem, you create a gritty shower

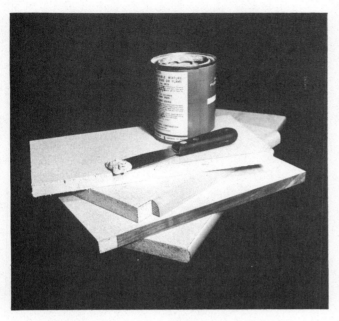

You can purchase some particleboard shelving with an edge-filled bullnose (bottom); you can glue or veneer tape (second from bottom); you can add solid moldings as shown previously; or you can sand smooth and fill with wood putty and sand.

Carbide tools are almost a must when working with particleboard. Unless you are doing a small job—and most cabinets are not small jobs—an investment in carbide-tipped saw blades and router bits is well worth the cost. (This and all following photos in Chapter 8 are courtesy of Louisiana-Pacific Corporation.)

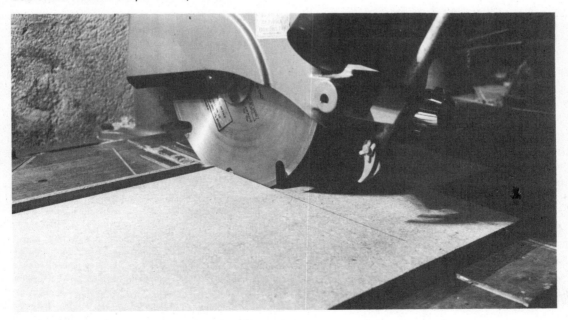

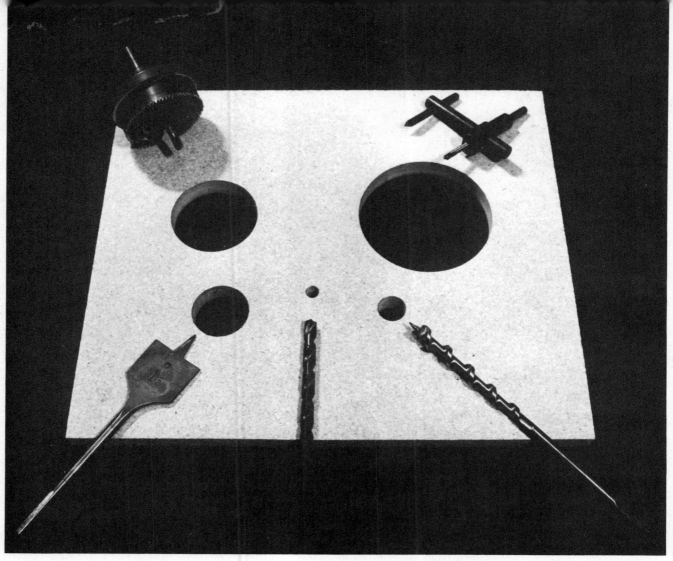

Particleboard can be sawed, drilled and shaped with regular woodworking equipment, either hand or powered. Particularly when drilling, however, it's important to supply a firm backing to prevent material from tearing-out on the back side.

of particles. Safety glasses or a face shield are a must. Second, because of the high concentration of abrasive resins in the particleboard, tools dull quickly. For larger projects, such as cabinets, it's worthwhile to get carbide-tipped saw blades, router bits and shaper cutters. These special tools work faster, make smoother cuts and stay sharp much longer. You'll find the carbide tools will stay sharp ten or more times longer when working regular wood and are a good investment.

Power bits, twist drills, hole saws and fly cutters, along with most standard woodworking tools, work beautifully with particleboard. Be sure to back up particleboard when drilling to prevent splintering on the back side. This is true of plywood or solid lumber as well.

While routing is easy on particleboard, you'll notice that the core is not as dense as the area near the surface; it may require filling before a finish is applied.

When you fill the edge of particleboard, make the filler a creamy consistency for the edges, but thin it to paint-like consistency for the faces. You can eliminate the need for filler on the edges by using solid stock, molding or veneer tape.

Fastening and Gluing

Be sure to provide maximum gluing surfaces when making joints in particleboard, as shown for half-lap, mitered and splined joints. Strengthen

Some typical rabbeted corner joints. It must be stressed that with particleboard there must be a mechanical fastening combined with glue, fastening; this means that the more glue surface you can provide, the better off you are.

Illustrated are mitered-corner systems that reduce or eliminate the need for filling or finishing the rougher core material of particleboard. From top to bottom: interior glue block with a miter corner; splined miter corner; rabbeted-miter corner, all of which provide generous glue surfaces.

corner joints with inside glue blocks where possible. Nails are used only to hold the joints until the glue sets, as particleboard has very little nail-holding strength. Use finishing nails, countersink them, and cover the heads with wood putty. Wood screws are better than nails, as they are in any wood product, but sheet metal screws do best in particleboard. These screws have wider, deeper threads that "bite" into the particleboard. Either kind of screw for particleboard should be longer and thinner than you would use in solid lumber. Turn the screws in firmly, but don't overdo it or you'll strip the threads. A drop of white glue in each screw hole helps. The glue seals the particleboard and enables the threads to make a more solid cut in the material.

Nail heads and screw heads are countersunk and covered with wood putty that is sanded smooth when dry. As an alternative to putty, counterbore the holes and then fill the recesses with short plugs or pieces of dowel, or wooden "buttons" that create a "colonial" look. Where joints are to be occasionally taken apart, use plated finishing washers under the screw heads.

Fastening hardware and finishing techniques, left to right: finishing nail, wood screw both countersunk and puttied over; wood screw with finishing cup washer; Tee-Nut and machine screw; sheet metal screw with button to cover counterbored sheet metal screw; sheet metal screw with head in counterbored hole that is then plugged with length of dowel or cut plug. At right is a plug cutter that can be used in a drill press or portable drill to create plugs from stock being used.

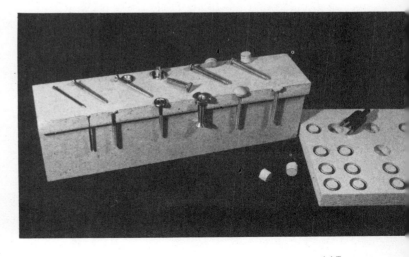

When you join two pieces of particleboard so that only one side will be exposed . . . such as rails and stiles in doors or cabinet frames . . . corrugated fasteners or "Skotch" fasteners can be used, along with glue. Remember that all particleboard joints that are to be permanent must include glue.

Any hardware that can be used with plywood or solid lumber can be used with particleboard. Pulls and handles used for doors and drawers, however, should be the "bolt-through" type rather than being screwed to the surface. If that is necessary, use sheet metal rather than wood screws. Surface-mount the hinges; don't screw them to the edges of particleboard. It takes only 160 pounds of pull to remove a sheet metal from edges of particleboard, but 225 pounds to wrench it from the face.

Hinges, pulls and other standard hardware used on wood and plywood can be applied to particleboard projects. However, where wood screws are normally used. As for attaching hinges, sheet metal screws are recommended.

Paint can be applied to particleboard with brush or roller, or by means of a spray gun. Oil-base paints or lacquers are preferred over latex-base paints that tend to raise the grain and create a rough surface. While particleboard has no true grain, it is a wood product and the various particles do swell when wet.

9 Applying Plastic Laminate

High-pressure plastic laminate is used on most countertops, and is available in a wide variety of solid colors, as well as patterns and even woodgrains. The laminate is made by assembling layers of paper and chemicals, then subjecting this "sandwich" to tremendous heat and pressure. The result is a dense, long-wearing material that is easily cleaned.

Like any material, however, after a number of years it begins to show signs of wear; it becomes scratched and dull and there may even be bulges and bubbles. You can replace the doors on your cabinets with new ones, and paint or stain the facings, but an old base counter never will look good until you replace the plastic laminate.

Much has been said about renewing laminate, and the problem of removing the old contact adhesive from the plywood or particleboard contact once you have stripped off the old laminate. Removing the laminate is fairly simple: you just find a loose edge, slip a putty knife under it and start pulling.

The problem is with the adhesive. Unfortunately, up to now, there has been no really good way to remove the old adhesive. If you apply new adhesive over the old, you never really get a good bond, and the new laminate will start to come loose and will buckle within days after you try this stunt.

The only practical renovation is to completely

Planked Hickory Woodgrain pattern is a beautiful way to add the easy-care durability of high-pressure laminated plastic to your kitchen, while complementing the natural beauty of hardwood cabinets. (Photo courtesy of Wilsonart)

Close-up of sink that was renewed by replacing countertop and new plastic laminate. Backsplash also is covered with wood-grain plastic laminate.

Tools required for replacing countertop include electric jig saw, portable router (or hand laminate trimmer), electric drill, hand saw, file, screwdriver and hammer.

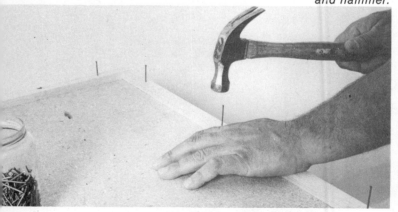

After ¾-inch particleboard or plywood is cut to size of countertop, strips of 1 × 2 stock are nailed to edge to create thickness of 1½ inches.

replace the countertop. There are two ways countertops are attached; (1) with wood screws countersunk down through the top, and the screw heads are exposed when you pry off the old laminate; (2) with screws driven up through the framing into the underside of the top. This latter is actually the better method, whether the top is plywood or particleboard.

Either method of attaching the top, however, works; the choice really is up to you. The main advantage of the screws being driven from underneath is that you can get at them to tighten or loosen them, which might be necessary if you wanted to shim up one corner or end of the countertop to level it. If the laminate has already been applied, the screw heads are covered and there is nothing you can do.

To get back to renewing a countertop: if it is a sink counter, shut off the water and disconnect the water lines and drain. Pry off the laminate, if necessary, to get at the screws holding the top to the framing. You can use the old top as a pattern, if you wish the exact dimensions again. You may decide, however, that you want more or less overhang on the top.

Once you have decided, cut the top to size from plywood or particleboard, then glue and nail on 1 × 2 strips around the edge (or variations of this as detailed in the chapter on kitchen cabinets). Tools you will need for renewing the countertop are those found in most home workshops. You can save on a lot of cutting by having the lumberyard cut the top material to the sizes you have already determined. This also makes it easier to haul the materials home. If you have a portable router, you can purchase a special plastic-laminate cutting setup. If not, you can use a hand-powered trimmer with carbide cutters in it. Files also can be used, if you trim the laminate to about 1/8 inch oversize, then file it down. We'd recommend the manual trimmer. They are not too expensive and will last a lifetime; you probably will have a laminate job every few years and the tool will save time and trouble.

As described in chapter 1, most countertops are about 24 inches wide. To renew a countertop you purchase laminate 30 inches wide, and a foot or two longer than you think necessary, to allow for waste and trimming. Cut the laminate on a table or radial-arm saw, using a slightly dull plywood-cutting blade. Wear safety goggles, or better still, a face shield. The particles of laminate flying back in your face can be irritating if not painful, and definitely hazardous to your eyes.

Cut a strip about 1/8 inch wider than the edge of the countertop you have created including the strips along the edges. Check the fit, then apply contact adhesive to the laminate and countertop edge. Follow the instructions on the adhesive container, which may say to wait a few minutes, or half an hour. There also will be listed a maximum time, after which the adhesive will not hold. Should you manage not to apply the laminate within this time limit, simply apply another coat on both the countertop and the laminate and redo the job.

Press the laminate firmly against the edge of the top, then go along with a block of wood and hammer and tap firmly to make sure the laminate adheres. Even better, use a flat roller that will squeeze out air bubbles and assure a full contact of the laminate.

Strip for edge is cut and applied first. It is allowed to project slightly above top surface of new counter top. It is applied with contact adhesive.

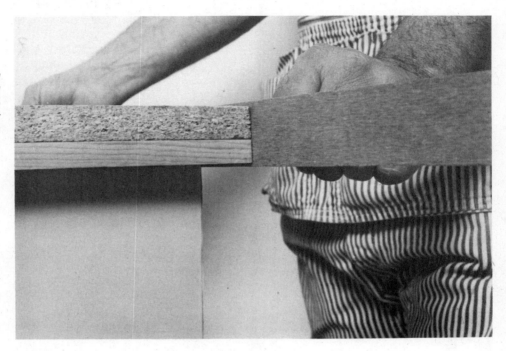

If you have portable router with laminate cutter, it can be used to trim upper edge of laminate flush with top of counter. Fine file also can be used, if held flat on countertop.

Use a router with laminate trimmer, or a hand trimmer, and cut the top edge of the laminate flush with the countertop. Next, cut the laminate pieces for the countertop, allowing at least 1/8 inch extra in width and length. Check the fit, then apply the adhesive.

Because of the large surface, you need help in aligning the laminate before pressing it onto the adhesive. Use dowels or metal welding rods between the countertop and laminate until you have the laminate properly aligned, then remove the supports one at a time as you press the laminate to the countertop. This method is easier and better than using newspaper or wrapping paper, as is sometimes suggested, because too often the paper will stick to the glue in spots.

Trim the edge of the laminate on the top as you did on the edge, using the same tools and methods.

Plastic laminate is cut about ¼ inch oversize for top of counter, and then positioned to make sure it is the proper size. It then is removed and contact adhesive is applied to back of the laminate and the top of counter. On plywood or particleboard, it's a good idea to apply two coats of adhesive, as the wood products are somewhat porous.

After adhesive is applied, plastic laminate is placed on countertop, but kept above it by small-diameter dowels or pieces of welding rod to prevent adhesive "grabbing" until you have the piece positioned correctly.

Backsplash is covered separately, then holes are drilled through so wood screws can pass through it and be driven into the back edge of countertop. Apply latex calking to the back edge of the countertop so there will be a waterproof seal between it and back splash.

Router with special laminate cutter can be used to trim laminate on the top flush with edge strips. It also can be filed, or trimmed with hand-powered laminate trimmer.

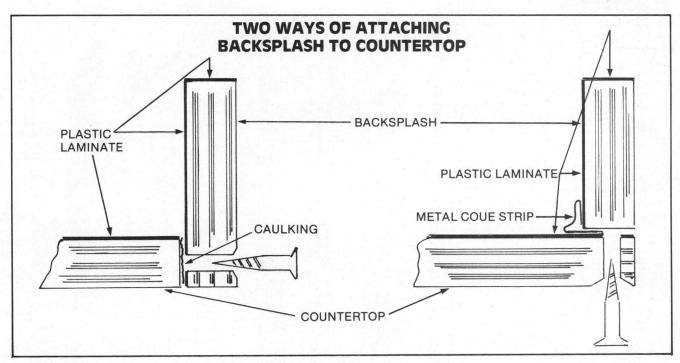

TWO WAYS OF ATTACHING
BACKSPLASH TO COUNTERTOP

PLASTIC LAMINATE

BACKSPLASH

PLASTIC LAMINATE

METAL COUE STRIP

CAULKING

COUNTERTOP

Backsplash is covered with laminate separately, then is attached with screws before counter is attached to frame by driving screws from underneath. Caulking or metal strip is used between counter and backsplash.

Use the original countertop to determine the size of the hole for the sink. If a new sink is to be installed, get proper size from instructions that come with it. Drill your starting hole inside the outline you draw.

Sink cutout is made with portable electric jig saw. Make sure the sole of the saw is clean and has no burrs that might mar the surface of the new laminate.

If you have a back splash on the countertop that will also be covered with laminate, cover it separately, then attach it to the back edge or top (as described in the chapter on kitchen counters). Clearance holes for the screws are drilled through the plywood or particleboard and the laminate, so the back splash can be attached. A bead of caulking should be applied along the edge of the back splash to seal it against water.

A cutout is required for the sink, and you can use the old counter top for a pattern, or perhaps you will want to locate the sink differently. Mark the outline, drill a hole in each corner, then cut out the opening with a portable electric jig saw.

Replace the sink by just reversing the steps for taking it out. Turn on the water and check and repair any leaks, and do the same with the drain.

Since your plastic laminate required replacing, it is quite likely the sink is chipped, beat and battered, and should be replaced. This is not a difficult job and, since you already have the old sink removed, half the job is already done. As with many household appliances, sinks now are designed for do-it-yourself installation. One such sink is the "Neptune Lifetime Sink." The stainless-steel unit shown on the following page illustrates simple step-by-step installation.

Complete instructions are packaged with this sink, as with others for the do-it-yourself homeowner, so be sure to study them carefully. The cutout for the new sink will be described, and in some cases a paper template will be in the instructions to be marked out directly onto the countertop.

Check sink in opening to make sure it fits properly; file off any projects or rough spots. Apply caulking around edge of cutout, then re-install sink. Or install new one as per instructions.

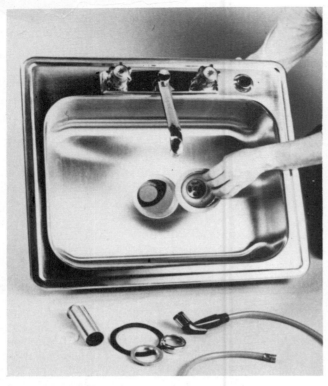

Do-it-yourself stainless-steel sink installation starts with you mounting faucet, spray and drain fittings before the sink is even fitted in the opening in the countertop. (Photo series courtesy of Neptune Lifetime Sinks)

Step two is to fit into the sink rim the "one-hand" mounting clips. A continuous head of caulking then is applied to the underside of the rim.

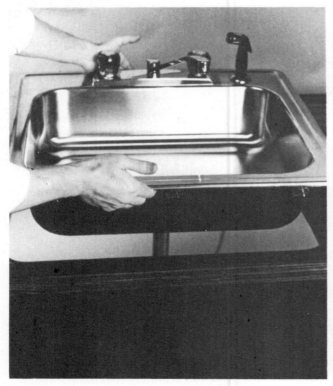

Lower the sink into the countertop cutout. It might be handy to have someone help with this part of the operation.

With the sink in the cutout, position the clips, then tighten them with a screwdriver. Make sure caulking squeezes out under the complete rim on the countertop. Wipe off the excess, then make the plumbing and drain connections.

Manufacturer's List

Softwood lumber for framing, and plywood for building cabinets, plus a limited selection of hardwood-plywood and hardwood, can be purchased from local lumberyards and home centers. If you want to use fairly exotic hardwoods for framing, or hardwood plywoods such as oak, walnut and similar, you'll have to buy them from mail-order houses who cater to home craftpersons who build fine furniture and cabinets. We strongly recommend that you send for catalogs from the various outlets listed, then peruse the many kinds of lumber, plywood, and specialty hardware, before making your selection.

Addresses of various companies who provided photographs are listed; if you write to them they will send you colorful brochures as well as names and addresses of dealers in your area. If you build cabinets in any room in the house, you may also wish to put down a new flooring material or wall paneling; addresses for these companies are included.

Furniture-Grade Hardwoods and Hardwood Plywoods, Specialty Hardware

Albert Constantine and Son, 2050 Eastchester Road, Bronx, NY 10461. Catalog 50¢

Craftsman Wood Service, 2727 S. Mary Street, Chicago, IL 60608, catalog 50¢

Educational Lumber Co., P.O. Box 5373, Asheville, NC 28803, catalog 50¢

Minnesota Woodworkers Supply Co., Rogers, MN 55374, catalog 50¢

Companies and Associations Listed in the Text

American Olean Tile, Lansdale, PA 19446

American Plywood Assocation, P.O. Box 2277, Tacoma, WA 98401

Armstrong Cork Company, Lancaster, PA 17604

Aster Products

Azrock Floor Products, P.O. Box 531, San Antonio, TX 78292

Clopay Corporation, Clopay Square, Cincinnati, OH 45214

Flexalum Decor Blinds, Hunter Douglas Inc., 20 Campus Road, Totowa, NJ 07512

Georgia-Pacific Corporation, 900 S. W. 5th Avenue, Portland, OR 97204

Kinkead Industries, Subsidiary of US Gypsum Company, 101 South Wacker Drive, Chicago, IL 60606

Louisiana-Pacific Corporation, 1300 S. W. Fifth Avenue. Portland, OR 97201

Marlite Division, Masonite Corporation, Dover, OH 44622

Mary Carter Paint Company, 1191 South Wheeling Road, Wheeling, IL 60090

Masonite Corporation, 29 N. Wacker Drive, Chicago, IL 60606

National Gypsum Company, First International Building, Dallas, TX 75270

Neptune Lifetime Sinks, 1801 West 19th Street, Broadview, IL 60153

Readybuilt Products Company, P.O. Box 4306, Baltimore, MD 21223

Thomas Strahan Wallcovering Division, US Gypsum Company, 101 South Wacker Drive, Chicago, IL 60606

Tile Council of America, P.O. Box 503, Mahwah, NJ 07430

Wallcovering Industry Bureau, P.O. Box 503, Mahwah, NJ 07430

Wall-Tex Div., Borden Chemical Company, 7th & Grant Avenue, Columbus, OH 43216

Western Wood Moulding and Millwork Producers, P.O. Box 25278, Portland, OR 97225

Wisonart, 2800 W. Lancaster, Ft. Worth, TX 76107

U.S. Plywood, Division of Champion International, 777 Third Avenue, New York, NY 10017

Index

Other SUCCESSFUL Books

SUCCESSFUL PLANTERS, Orcutt. "Definitive book on container gardening." *Philadelphia Inquirer*. Build a planter, and use it for a room divider, a living wall, a kitchen herb garden, a centerpiece, a table, an aquarium—and don't settle for anything that looks homemade! Along with construction steps, there is advice on the best types of planters for individual plants, how to locate them for best sun and shade, and how to provide the best care to keep plants healthy and beautiful, inside or outside the home. 8½" x 11"; 136 pp; over 200 photos and illustrations. Cloth $12.00. Paper $4.95.

BOOK OF SUCCESSFUL FIREPLACES, 20th ed., Lytle. The expanded, updated edition of the book that has been a standard of the trade for over 50 years—over a million copies sold! Advice is given on selecting from the many types of fireplaces available, on planning and adding fireplaces, on building fires, on constructing and using barbecues. Also includes new material on wood as a fuel, woodburning stoves, and energy savings. 8½" x 11"; 128 pp; over 250 photos and illustrations. $5.95 Paper.

SUCCESSFUL ROOFING & SIDING, Reschke. "This well-illustrated and well-organized book offers many practical ideas for improving a home's exterior." *Library Journal*. Here is full information about dealing with contractors, plus instructions specific enough for the do-it-yourselfer. All topics, from carrying out a structural checkup to supplemental exterior work like dormers, insulation, and gutters, fully covered. Materials to suit all budgets and home styles are reviewed and evaluated. 8½" x 11"; 160 pp; over 300 photos and illustrations. $5.95 Paper. (Main selection Popular Science and McGraw-Hill Book Clubs)

PRACTICAL & DECORATIVE CONCRETE, Wilde. "Spells it all out for you...is good for beginner or talented amateur..." *Detroit Sunday News*. Complete information for the layman on the use of concrete inside or outside the home. The author—Executive Director of the American Concrete Institute—gives instructions for the installation, maintenance, and repair of foundations, walkways, driveways, steps, embankments, fences, tree wells, patios, and also suggests "fun" projects. 8½" x 11"; 144 pp; over 150 photos and illustrations. $12.00 Cloth. $4.95 Paper. (Featured alternate, Popular Science and McGraw-Hill Book Clubs)

SUCCESSFUL HOME ADDITIONS, Schram. For homeowners who want more room but would like to avoid the inconvenience and distress of moving, three types of home additions are discussed: garage conversion with carport added; bedroom, bathroom, sauna addition; major home renovation which includes the addition of a second-story master suite and family room. All these remodeling projects have been successfully completed and, from them, step-by-step coverage has been reported of almost all potential operations in adding on to a home. The straightforward presentation of information on materials, methods, and costs, as well as a glossary of terms, enables the homeowner to plan, arrange contracting, or take on some of the work personally in order to cut expenses. 8½" x 11"; 144 pp; over 300 photos and illustrations. Cloth $12.00. Paper $5.95.

FINISHING OFF, Galvin. A book for both the new-home owner buying a "bonus space" house, and those who want to make use of previously unused areas of their homes. The author advises which jobs can be handled by the homeowner, and which should be contracted out. Projects include: putting in partitions and doors to create rooms; finishing off floors and walls and ceilings; converting attics and basements; designing kitchens and bathrooms, and installing fixtures and cabinets. Information is given for materials that best suit each job, with specifics on tools, costs, and building procedures. 8½" x 11"; 144 pp; over 250 photos and illustrations. Cloth $12.00. Paper $5.95.

SUCCESSFUL FAMILY AND RECREATION ROOMS, Cornell. How to best use already finished rooms or convert spaces such as garage, basement, or attic into family/recreation rooms. Along with basics like lighting, ventilation, plumbing, and traffic patterns, the author discusses "mood setters" (color schemes, fireplaces, bars, etc.) and finishing details (flooring, wall covering, ceilings, built-ins, etc.) A special chapter gives quick ideas for problem areas. 8½" x 11"; 144 pp; over 250 photos and diagrams. (Featured alternate for McGraw-Hill Book Clubs.) $12.00 Cloth. $4.95 Paper.

SUCCESSFUL HOME GREENHOUSES, Scheller. Instructions, complete with diagrams, for building all types of greenhouses. Among topics covered are: site location, climate control, drainage, ventilation, use of sun, auxiliary equipment, and maintenance. Charts provide characteristics and requirements of plants and greenhouse layouts are included in appendices. "One of the most completely detailed volumes of advice for those contemplating an investment in a greenhouse." *Publishers Weekly*. 8½" x 11"; 136 pp; over 200 photos and diagrams. (Featured alternates of the Popular Science and McGraw-Hill Book Clubs). $12.00 Cloth. $4.95 Paper.

SUCCESSFUL SPACE SAVING AT HOME, Galvin. The conquest of inner space in apartments, whether tiny or ample, and homes, inside and out. Storage and built-in possibilities for all living areas, with a special section of illustrated tips from the professional space planners. 8½" x 11"; 128 pp; over 150 B-W and color photographs and illustrations. $12.00 Cloth. $4.95 Paper.

SUCCESSFUL KITCHENS, 2nd ed., Galvin. Updated and revised edition of the book *Workbench* called "A thorough and thoroughly reliable guide to all phases of kitchen design and construction. Special features include how to draw up your own floor plan and cabinet arrangement, plus projects such as installing countertops, dishwashers, cabinets, flooring, lighting, and more. 8½"x11"; 144 pp; over 250 photos and illustrations, incl. color. Cloth $12.00. Paper $5.95.

SUCCESSFUL LIVING ROOMS, Hedden. A collection of projects to beautify and add enjoyment to living and dining areas. The homeowner will be able to build a bar, dramatize lighting, enhance or brighten up an old fireplace, build entertainment centers, and make structural changes. "The suggestions…are imaginative. A generous number of illustrations make the book easy to understand. Directions are concisely written…new ideas, superior presentation." *Library Journal.* 8½"x11"; 152 pp; over 200 illustrations and photos, incl. color. Cloth $12.00. Paper $5.95.

SUCCESSFUL LANDSCAPING, Felice. Tips and techniques on planning and caring for lawns, trees, shrubs, flower and vegetable gardens, and planting areas. "Profusely illustrated…this book can help those looking for advice on improving their home grounds. Thorough details." *Publishers Weekly.* "Comprehensive handbook." *American Institute of Landscape Architects.* Also covers building fences, decks, bird baths and feeders, plus climate-and-planting schedules, and a glossary of terms and chemical products. 8½"x11"; 128 pp; over 200 illustrations including color; $12.00 Cloth. $4.95 Paper.

IMPROVING THE OUTSIDE OF YOUR HOME, Schram. This complete guide to an attractive home exterior at low cost covers every element, from curb to chimney to rear fence. Emphasis is on house facade and attachments, with tips on enhancing natural settings and adding manmade features. Basic information on advantages or disadvantages of materials plus expert instructions make it easy to carry out repairs and improvements that increase the home's value and reduce its maintenance. 8½"x11"; 168 pp; over 250 illustrations including color; $12.00 Cloth. $5.95 Paper.

SUCCESSFUL LOG HOMES, Ritchie. Log homes are becoming increasingly popular—low cost, ease of construction and individuality being their main attractions. This manual tells how to work from scratch whether cutting or buying logs—or how to remodel an existing log structure—or how to build from a prepackaged kit. The author advises on best buys, site selection, evaluation of existing homes, and gives thorough instructions for building and repair. 8½"x11"; 168 pp; more than 200 illustrations including color. $12.00 Cloth. $5.95 Paper.

SUCCESSFUL SMALL FARMS—BUILDING PLANS & METHODS, Leavy. A comprehensive guide that enables the owner of a small farm to plan, construct, add to, or repair buildings at least expense and without disturbing his production. Emphasis is on projects the farmer can handle without a contractor, although advice is given on when and how to hire work out. Includes basics of farmstead layout, livestock housing, environmental controls, storage needs, fencing, building construction and preservation, and special needs. 8½"x11"; 192 pp; over 250 illustrations. $14.00 Cloth. $5.95 Paper.

SUCCESSFUL HOME REPAIR—WHEN *NOT* TO CALL THE CONTRACTOR. Anyone can cope with household repairs or emergencies using this detailed, clearly written book. The author offers tricks of the trade, recommendations on dealing with repair crises, and step-by-step repair instructions, as well as how to set up a preventive maintenance program. 8½"x11"; 144 pp; over 150 illustrations. $12.00 Cloth. $4.95 Paper.

OUTDOOR RECREATION PROJECTS, Bright. Transform you backyard into a relaxation or game area—without enormous expense—using the instructions in this book. There are small-scale projects such as putting greens, hot tubs, or children's play areas, plus more ambitious ventures including tennis courts and skating rinks. Regional differences are considered; recommendations on materials, construction methods are given as are estimated costs. "Will encourage you to build the patio you've always wanted, install a tennis court or boat dock, or construct playground equipment…Bright provides information on choosing tools, selecting lumber, and paving with concrete, brick or stone." *House Beautiful.* (Featured alternate Popular Science and McGraw-Hill Book Clubs). 8½"x11"; 160 pp; over 200 photos and illustrations including color. $12.00 Cloth. $5.95 Paper.

SUCCESSFUL WOOD BOOK—HOW TO CHOOSE, USE, AND FINISH EVERY TYPE OF WOOD, Bard. Here is the primer on wood—how to select it and use it effectively, efficiently, and safely—for all who want to panel a wall, build a house frame, make furniture, refinish a floor, or carry out any other project involving wood inside or outside the home. The author introduces the reader to wood varieties and their properties, describes major wood uses, advises on equipping a home shop, and covers techniques for working with wood including the use of paints and stains. 8½"x11"; 160 pp; over 250 illustrations including color. $12.00 Cloth. $5.95 Paper.

SUCCESSFUL PET HOMES, Mueller. "There are years worth of projects…The text is good and concise—all around, I am most impressed." *Roger Caras, Pets and Wildlife, CBS.* "A thoroughly delightful and helpful book for everyone who loves animals." *Syndicated reviewer, Lisa Oglesby.* Here is a new approach to keeping both pet owners and pets happy by choosing, buying, building functional but inexpensive houses, carriers, feeders, and play structures for dogs, cats, and birds. The concerned pet owner will find useful advice on providing for pet needs with the least wear and tear on the home. 8½"x11"; 116 pp; over 200 photos and illustrations. Cloth $12.00. $4.95 Paper.